Cow Country

COW
COUNTRY

by Edward Everett Dale

UNIVERSITY OF OKLAHOMA PRESS
NORMAN

BY EDWARD EVERETT DALE

Territorial Acquisitions of the United States
(Privately printed, 1912)
Tales of the Tepee (Boston, 1919)
A History of Oklahoma (with J. S. Buchanan) (Chicago, 1924)
Letters of Lafayette (Oklahoma City, 1925)
The Problem of Indian Administration
(with Meriam and others) (Baltimore, 1928)
The Prairie Schooner and other Poems (Guthrie, 1929)
Outline and References for Oklahoma History
(with M. L. Wardell) (Privately printed, 1929)
Readings in Oklahoma History (with J. L. Rader)
(Chicago, 1930)
Frontier Trails (ed.) (Boston, 1930)
Grant Foreman: A Brief Biography (Norman, 1933)
A Rider of the Cherokee Strip (ed.) (Boston, 1936)
Cherokee Cavaliers (with Gaston Litton) (Norman, 1939)
History of the United States
(with Dwight L. Dumond and Edgar B. Wesley) (Boston, 1948)
History of Oklahoma (with M. L. Wardell) (New York, 1948)
Oklahoma: The Story of a State (Evanston, 1949)
The Indians of the Southwest (Norman, 1949)
Pioneer Judge (with James D. Morrison) (Cedar Rapids, 1958)
Frontier Ways (Austin, 1959)
The Range Cattle Industry (Norman, 1930; New Edition,
Norman, 1960)
Cow Country (Norman, 1942; New Edition, Norman, 1965)

To

My Brother George

Top hand and senior partner

in our old ranching firm

of Dale Brothers

Preface

URING MY LIFETIME THE CATTLE industry has passed through a number of phases, one of the most colorful of which I have recorded in this book. The book also might be said to have grown from a series of phases of my life. Some of it was gleaned from my experiences in riding the range as a cowhand and small ranchman in western Oklahoma for some five or six years beginning in my late teens.

Many years later, while I was a graduate student at Harvard, the memories of these earlier days were no doubt an important factor in determining the choice of "The Range Cattle Industry in Oklahoma" as the subject of my doctoral dissertation. The work done under the direction of Professor Frederick Jackson Turner was completed and the degree conferred in 1922.

The fact that my thesis for the Ph.D. at Harvard was on the history of ranching in Oklahoma must have attracted the attention of some official in the U.S. Department of Agriculture. At any rate, early in 1924 the chief of the Division of Historical and Statistical Research in the Bureau of Agricultural Economics asked me to accept a temporary appointment in that division to write a history of the range cattle industry in Western America from 1865 to 1924. My work on this study was begun in Washington in August, 1924, and completed in June, 1925.

A year later, the University of Oklahoma, in which I was a member of the faculty of the department of history, granted me a year's leave of absence so that I might accept an invitation to join the staff of the Meriam Commission of the Institute for Government Research that was to make a survey of conditions among the American Indians.

The survey group consisted of eight men and two women. Each had a special field for investigation, mine being economic conditions with emphasis upon the sources of the Indians' income. We spent over eight months in the field, beginning in November, 1926. During this time we traveled in virtually all states west of the Mississippi and those east of it which had any significant number of Indians.

My part of the work brought me into contact with the livestock men who looked after the tribal herds of cattle on a number of the large western reservations. It also gave me the opportunity to talk with many white ranchmen who leased large areas of certain reservations for grazing cattle. My association with these men not only sustained my interest in ranching but gave me considerable information concerning the problems of the cattlemen in western states from Arizona to Montana. Some of this appears in the Miriam Commission's final report, *The Problems of Indian Administration*, published by the Johns Hopkins Press in 1928. By the time the first draft of the report had been completed, it was necessary for me to return to my regular job at the University of Oklahoma.

In the meantime the manuscript I had prepared in Washington on the range cattle industry had been read by interested officials of the U.S. Department of Agriculture. Eventually it was released to the University of Oklahoma Press, which published it in 1930 under the title, *The Range Cattle Industry*. The comparatively small edition was soon exhausted, and over the years copies became so scarce that the volume was classed as "exceedingly rare" by rare-book dealers. To meet the demand for it, the University of Oklahoma Press issued a second edition in 1960.

The book is an intensive economic study of the cattle industry in the West from 1865 to 1924. It was written largely from manuscript sources and government documents, contains a number of rare maps and illustrations, and is heavily documented. To my regret, limitations of space made it necessary to omit much material of human interest, as well as accounts of the colorful characters who made the Cow Country and the comedy and tragedy in their lives.

Some of these facets had been included in articles of mine published in historical journals or in papers read at historical society meetings. Then, about 1940, it occurred to me that these articles and lectures might be brought together and published as a book.

This proved not practical; therefore, the only chapters which had been published prior to book publication are chapters two, eight, nine, and ten. All others were written specifically for this book. The verses at the beginning of each chapter are fragments of my own rhymes never published elsewhere. The first edition of *Cow Country* was released by the University of Oklahoma Press in April, 1942. A second printing was made in June, 1943, and a third in August, 1945.

The volume was soon out of print, and eventually the difficulty of securing a copy even at five times the original price brought an insistent demand for another edition. As a result, the University of Oklahoma Press decided to reissue the little book as a volume in the flourishing and very successful Western Frontier Library.

For this I wish to express my sincere thanks to the staff of the University of Oklahoma Press. I also wish to express my appreciation to the editors of the *Mississippi Valley Historical Review*, *Agricultural History*, *The Chronicles of Oklahoma*, and the *Proceedings of the Southwestern Political and Social Sciences Association* for permission to republish the four chapters which first appeared in these publications. In addition, special thanks are due Mr. Richard G. Underwood for the decorative sketches at chapter openings and to my wife, Rosalie, who typed the original manuscript more than twenty years ago and, in the absence of my secretary, typed this introduction.

EDWARD EVERETT DALE

Norman, Oklahoma,
October 12, 1964

Contents

Part I

A Potential Pasture Land

I

The Basis of the Cow Country

Give me the plains
Where it seldom rains
And the wind forever blows;
It is there I would be
Though there's never a tree
And the farther you look
The less you see
For there's where the beefsteak grows.

PLAINS SONG

WHEN THE WAR BETWEEN THE STATES came to a close in 1865 agricultural settlement had occupied only the first tier of states beyond the Mississippi and, with the exception of Texas and Kansas, had barely started in the second.

Between this line forming the western edge of settlement and the base of the Rockies lies a vast region of plains traversed by a number of broad, sandy rivers usually flowing in a southeasterly direction into the Mississippi or its great western tributary, the Missouri. Along these streams and their affluents were narrow fringes of timber and in a few areas were small groves, open forests of scraggly mesquite, or patches of scrub oak, but the greater part of the entire region was a more or less level plain covered before the coming of the plow with a rich coat of grass, in some places thickly sprinkled with colorful wild flowers. It slopes gradually upward to the base of the Rockies and in some places is six or seven thousand feet above sea level. The climate is on the whole dry, for while the rainfall in eastern Kansas or Oklahoma may be as much as forty inches a year, it steadily decreases to fifteen inches or less in the region just east of the mountains.

3

It was an ideal pasture land in 1865 and for many years thereafter, and nature had moreover provided it with an abundant supply of animals to consume the grass. Over much of it roamed countless numbers of the American bison, commonly called buffalo.

The discovery of gold in California in 1848 had sent many thousands of people adventuring across the plains in search of wealth. These, together with the emigrants to Oregon, the Santa Fe traders, and the Mormons, had before 1865 established several well-defined trails across the plains, which had tended to divide the buffalo into two great groups, or herds, a division further emphasized by the building of the Pacific Railway completed in 1869.

The buffalo were, however, by no means the only grass-consuming animals in the Great Plains region. Large numbers of the prong-horned antelope were found in many places, while along the streams and among the brush-covered sand hills were many deer. To these must be added the innumerable prairie dogs and jack rabbits that in some areas doubtless ate more herbage than did the larger animals.

In spite of the abundant pasturage, however, life was not always easy for these herbivorous animals. Cold winters accompanied by sleet and snow doubtless took heavy toll of the buffalo herds at times as they later did of the herds of cattle. Beasts of prey also must live and these were in certain areas quite numerous. They included not only the sneaking coyote, preying chiefly upon rabbits, prairie dogs, and birds, but not averse to dining on a young fawn or a buffalo calf, but also the larger wolf, sometimes called the "lobo," capable of pulling down a half-grown buffalo. In addition to these were the panthers, or mountain lions, and "bob cats" commonly called catamounts.

Even before the coming of the whites, however, the chief enemy of the game animals which roamed the plains was man. For many Indian tribes of this region, the buffalo was the chief source of food, clothing, and shelter. Not only was buffalo meat their staple article of food, but from the hides were made clothing, moccasins, robes for covering at night, and the round tent called a tepee, which served as a home. From the horns were constructed spoons, cups, and ladles; the sinews were used in sewing, and from the bones were fashioned awls and needles.

The Indians who occupied this region included many stocks and tribes. In western Texas, extending north into Oklahoma, were the fierce Comanches. They were very war-like, raided in Mexico, and attacked the settlements of the Anglo-American settlers of Texas. No tribe in the West was more dreaded by the pioneer settlers and perhaps none was more difficult to subdue. Proud, haughty, and very intelligent, a remarkable horseman, and apparently an inveterate foe of the whites, the Comanche was long the scourge of the southwestern frontier.

To the north of the Comanches largely in Oklahoma, Kansas, and Colorado, and at times in northern Texas, were the Kiowas, a somewhat smaller tribe than the Comanche. They were also a very intelligent people, but although they were quite warlike and had several notable leaders they did not on the whole prove nearly so troublesome as did the first named tribe.

North and east of the Kiowas lived the Osages, of Siouan stock—tall, powerful Indians as are most Sioux. Their original home was Missouri though they also claimed most of eastern Oklahoma and extended their operations west into Kansas. They had early come in contact with the white traders since the Chouteaus, a family of French origin who dominated the fur trade, and others had established trade relations with them before the dawn of the nineteenth century. Like the other Plains Indians they owned many horses, hunted buffalo, and lived in round tepees of buffalo skin.

Northwest of the Osages were the Cheyennes, divided into northern and southern groups, the former occupying a great hunting ground in Montana, Dakota, and Wyoming, while the latter ranged largely in eastern Colorado and western Kansas and extended south into Oklahoma. They with their kinsmen, the Arapahoes, were of Algonquian stock and both tribes were "horse Indians," counting their wealth in their numerous ponies. They were a fighting tribe, often on the warpath though they too had early established relations with the white traders, notably the Bents, who had founded Bent's Fort near the site of the present town of LaJunta, Colorado, in the early thirties, and who bartered beads, red cloth, blankets, gunpowder, and whisky for furs and buffalo robes.

Most of the northern plains region was occupied by tribes of the great Siouan stock. These included the Tetons, Sans Arcs, Miniconjous, Hunkpapas, Oglalas, and a number of others. In many respects they resembled in their culture, way of life, and physical characteristics, their kinsmen, the Osages, or the Algonquian Cheyennes. They were predatory, warlike, subsisted largely upon the buffalo, and early engaged in trade with the Spanish, French, or American *voyageurs*, coming up the Missouri River from St. Louis, or with British traders of the Northwest Fur Company, or the Hudson's Bay Company from Canada, with which the first named company was merged in 1821.

Along the Loup Fork of the Platte and south of that

stream lived the Pawnees, dwelling in villages of earth-covered lodges. They were also hunters though they cultivated the soil more than did most other Plains tribes, raising crops of corn, beans, and squashes. Their kinsmen, the Wichitas, were largely in Oklahoma and were a semisedentary tribe occupying villages of grass lodges about which lay their little fields.

To the west of the Sioux in Montana were the Blackfeet, one of the fiercest and most warlike tribes in North America. Their territory extended up to the foot of the mountains, but they hunted buffalo on the plains and had many of the characteristics of other Plains tribes farther east.

A number of smaller tribes were to be found in the plains region and in the period from 1820 to 1840 many small tribes from east of the Mississippi were driven west and given reservations, not a few of them within the limits of the present state of Kansas. West of the mountains in the valleys between the different ranges, or in the area of the Great Basin, were many tribes including the Utes, Shoshones, Paiutes, and Washoes. In the far Southwest lived the peaceful Pueblos, Hopis, Pimas, and Papagos and their warlike neighbors, the Apaches and Navajos. These were real desert dwellers and their homeland, except in comparatively small areas subject to irrigation, is even today very thinly peopled by whites. This southwestern region has a history all its own as do the Great Basin and the vast area of the Rocky Mountain highland, which is not within the scope of this volume. It is true that they furnished pasturage for herds of cattle and sheep from the time of the coming of the early Spanish settlers in the seventeenth and eighteenth centuries, but for the purpose of this study the "Cow Country" is defined only as that region lying between the eastern base of the Rocky Mountains and the edge of agricultural settlement as it was about the time of the close of the War between the States.

Most of it had sufficient rainfall to produce a luxuriant growth of pasturage, and large parts of it especially in the eastern half were potentially valuable for the growing of crops. The grasses were of large variety. Along the streams and in the fertile valleys grew the tall bluestem while sage or bunch grass covered the looser soils and the low sand hills along the wide, and often nearly dry, rivers. Much of the area was, however, clothed with a thick coat of short, curling mesquite or buffalo grass. In consequence, the term "short grass country" was often loosely applied to most of this region and particularly to the western portion of it where a scanty rainfall made the herbage truly short, at least during much of the year.

This vast plains region is truly a land of magnificent distances. The first white men to enter it found that their standards of measurement must be increased. They must measure in feet instead of inches and miles instead of feet. It was, moreover, a land of paradoxes, a land where nature seemed to operate on a gigantic scale. The larger rivers were in time of flood raging torrents a mile or more in width, and in time of drought merely broad strips of sand with a narrow trickle of water near the center, and at times were entirely dry for many miles. The mountains which formed the western rim of the entire region were of enormous size as compared with even the highest peaks of the Appalachians. The summers were intensely hot and the winters in the northern portion bitterly cold. Long periods of drought were succeeded by torrential rains in which the clouds seemed literally to open and pour floods of water upon the parched earth. Scorching winds swept across the plains in summer and icy "northers" were common in winter. The strong wind was a feature to which Easterners found it difficult to accustom themselves. This gave rise to the familiar stock story of the man from New England who asked a native of the plains the question:

"Does the wind blow this way all the time?" only to receive the answer, "Hell no! It blows the other way about half the time."

Cyclones and electric storms were common. In the case of the latter the air sometimes became so heavily charged with electricity that the points of the horns of cattle would at night blaze with tiny tapers of light, and the tobacco-chewing cow hand who leaned over to spit was startled to see what looked like a ball of fire leap from his mouth. In the greater altitudes near the foot of the mountains the nights, even in midsummer, were often intensely cold though at midday the blazing sun seemed like a furnace.

The clearness and dryness of the atmosphere were noted by the earliest visitors. Wounds healed easily, almost never becoming infected. Meat cured readily and could be kept fresh for many days even in midsummer. Mirages were frequently observed by travelers, and one accustomed to the less clear and rarefied atmosphere farther east found himself grossly deceived by the apparent distance to a hill or mountain or other distant object. Often he would start to walk to a mountain believing it to be only half mile away when the distance might be ten times that much.

At the time of the outbreak of the War between the States, a considerable number of military posts had been established near the trails leading to the Pacific coast, or at strategic points in the Indian country to protect travelers and the miners operating in the Rocky Mountains or to keep down intertribal Indian wars. After the outbreak of the war, however, the garrisons from most of these were withdrawn, with the result that Indian troubles blazed up at various points. In Minnesota a major Indian outbreak developed which was put down only with great difficulty after a considerable loss of life.

Partially as a result of this, the government of the United States decided soon after the close of the War between the States upon a new Indian policy. At this time the Indians who had been driven to the West from the region east of the Mississippi (largely in the thirties), together with a few tribes indigenous to the area west of that river, had been given certain lands as reservations, but the majority of the warlike Plains tribes had merely made treaties of limits defining in a broad, general way their hunting grounds. It was now decided that these tribes should be rounded up and placed upon definite reservations set aside for them and compelled to remain there. This was not accomplished without war and bloodshed, for though the tribal leaders made treaties agreeing to accept clearly defined reservations, bands of restless younger men did not hesitate to leave the reservation and wander about over the plains, hunting buffalo and occasionally raiding on the white settlements, stealing horses, burning houses, and carrying off captives. When threatened by attack they hastened back to the lands set aside for them, where they were shielded and afforded protection even by the most tractable and peaceful members of the tribe. Within half a dozen years after Appomattox, however, most western tribes had been assigned reservations and a more or less determined effort was made to keep them there.

The Five Civilized Tribes, who at the time of removal were given virtually all of the present state of Oklahoma, had made an alliance with the Southern Confederacy and fought on the side of the South throughout the war. In consequence they were in 1866 compelled to give up the western half of their territory, a region approximately as large as Ohio, to furnish homes for some of these Plains tribes. Here a great reservation was set aside for the Kiowas and Comanches, another for the Cheyennes and Arapahoes, still a third for the Osages, and a number of smaller reservations for various other tribes. The great Cherokee Outlet, somewhat reduced in size by the creation of the Osage and other reservations but still including more than six million acres, remained as the property of its original owners, the Cherokees.

Far to the north in South Dakota were set aside huge reservations for the Sioux and Northern Cheyennes including the Pine Ridge, Rosebud, Brulé, and a number of others. Great reservations were also created in North Dakota and Montana, including that of the Blackfeet in the western part of the last named state. A considerable reservation was also established in Wyoming and a lesser one in Colorado. Enormous areas were included in the Indian reservations of the Southwest, especially in Arizona and New Mexico as well as in Utah, Nevada, and Idaho. These eventually furnished pasturage for large numbers of cattle and sheep but as has already been indicated such states, except for a part of New Mexico, lie largely outside the limits of the Cow Country as defined in this volume.

Each Indian reservation or, in the case of the smaller ones, group of reservations and the Indians who resided there were placed under the supervision and control of an official of the United States known as the Indian agent. It was his duty to prevent his charges from straying beyond the limits of the lands assigned to them, to see that they were properly cared for, and to attempt, at least, to teach them some of the rudiments of white civilization.

This was not easy. There was seldom much game on the reservation and while the government made some attempt to provide the Indians with food, the quantity furnished was never sufficient. In consequence, the temptation to leave his lands and stray away to hunt buffalo was often too much for the hungry Indian.

This temptation, however, was very soon removed by the guns of the white hunters. The close of the war had released from the armies of both North and South thousands of restless young men eager for any enterprise that promised profit and adventure. Many of these flocked to the western plains where some found employment in building the rapidly advancing western railways, others pushed on to the mountains to engage in mining, and not a few found in buffalo hunting a profitable though brief occupation. Buffalo hunters were also recruited from the ranks of the earlier trappers and fur traders who had found the supply of fur-bearing animals growing scarce, and from the men of various and sundry former vocations who naturally gravitated to the frontier.

Even before the outbreak of the war, it was estimated that more than one hundred thousand buffalo robes were marketed annually, and it seems certain that two or three times that number of animals were killed each year by the Indians and white frontiersmen for food or more or less wantonly by hunting parties. Soon after the close of the war, however, the systematic slaughter by professional hunters was accelerated. By the middle seventies buffalo were growing scarce on the southern plains and by the end of the decade they had virtually disappeared. The northern herd lasted two or three years longer, but by 1883 it too had been destroyed.

The rapid reduction and the final complete destruction of the buffalo herds not only left enormous areas of rich pasture lands without animals to consume the grass, but also made it possible to keep the Indians on their reservations and under control. With the complete disappearance of the buffalo these western Indians, formerly only partially dependent upon the government of the United States for food, became almost entirely so and in consequence were forced to accept the will of government officials or starve. To receive rations the Indians must remain on the reservation. As a result not only had these great buffalo ranges of the earlier days been left open to occupation by cattle, but the ranchman could now occupy them with herds with little fear of depredations on his animals or the loss of his own scalp at the hands of prowling bands of warriors. True, a hungry Indian did not differentiate too much between beef and the flesh of the buffalo, since he was apparently the originator of the idea expressed by the mountain men in the words "Meat's meat." Grazing on the reservations or near their borders would in all probability still entail the occasional loss of a few animals but the Indians were at least concentrated within definite limits where they could be watched and the strong hand of the agent which could give or withhold rations was a powerful instrument of control.

Moreover, the fact that the Indians must be fed created an important new market for beef. The Indian, accustomed for generations to subsisting largely upon the buffalo, demanded meat and this the government must supply. In consequence, the Indian Department of the government became the purchaser of many millions of pounds of beef annually to feed the reservation Indians. Naturally, the quantity of beef purchased by the United States for issue to the Indians constituted only a comparatively small part of that consumed annually by the people of the country as a whole. Yet, there can be no doubt that this market was a factor in promoting the growth of ranching on the plains and that a number of important cattlemen laid the foundations of their large enterprises by securing lucrative government contracts to supply Indians with beef.

It is clear then that the formation of the Cow Country was a natural and logical development in the economic history of the United States. The crop-growing farmers steadily moving westward for generations had occupied the first tier of states beyond the Mississippi by the time of the outbreak of the War between the States. Here the farmers had hesitated, daunted by the broad stretches of plains which lay beyond and which obviously could not be dealt with in the same fashion as could the more humid, wooded, or partially wooded regions farther east.

Yet the vast area beyond, extending to the foot of the Rocky Mountains, was an ideal pasture land which had for centuries supported millions of buffalo which had in turn furnished support for a sparse population of aboriginal people. With the destruction of the vast buffalo herds and the concentration of the Indians within comparatively narrow limits where they were subject to control, the land was wide open to occupation. It was therefore inevitable that men would appear eager to exploit the pastoral resources of this great region, while a crop-growing society, not yet in sore need of farm lands, was trying to make up its mind to tackle the problems presented by the occupation of a land so different from that to which it was accustomed.

The first of these men came out of a land to the south which scarcely more than two decades before had been an independent nation. This was Texas, a state which may be rightfully regarded as the root from which the Cow Country grew—a seed bin from which was drawn the grain for the planting of a vast pastoral empire.

Part II

Trailing North

II

Those Kansas Jayhawkers

I love the state of Texas,
The state where I was born,
Though I'm living now in Kansas
Where grows the tallest corn.
And I'm happy here in Kansas,
This sunny, wind-swept land,
But don't tell my folks in Texas
For they wouldn't understand.

THE TEXAN

IT WAS LATE IN THE SUMMER OF 1901
that a small party of us—all Texans—were taking a trainload
of cattle to Kansas City. There were half a dozen men in
the group. Among them was Ellison Carroll, onetime champion roper of the world. He had fourteen cars of three- and
four-year-old steers and was accompanied by two of his
cowboys. Also there was Jim Martin with a half dozen cars,
the author with four cars of "long twos," and finally Bill
Jones, a lean, lanky cowpuncher in charge of three cars for
his employer, a small ranchman of the South Panhandle.

It was a long and tiresome trip in the caboose of the cattle
train. There was little opportunity to get food, the weather
was hot, the road rough, and the seats uncomfortable. Conversation that had started out bravely enough began to
languish after twelve or fourteen hours. Men smoked cigarette after cigarette, or exercised their hungry jaws on large
quids of plug tobacco in lieu of food. Among the tobacco
chewers Bill Jones stood like Saul of old, "head and shoul-
ders above all Israel." Bill was a real ruminant animal, and
as he rolled his cud about in his mouth he expectorated
largely and frequently in the general direction of the cuspi-
dor, but apparently without any real ambition to hit the

target. Bill was merely snap shooting and finally seemed to forget the mark entirely and to fire completely at random.

At a division point some distance up in Kansas the train took the siding and a fresh crew came aboard. The new conductor bustled in, his hands full of papers, just as Bill delivered a particularly heavy barrage which seemed to have no objective whatever.

The train official frowned, glanced at numerous other small, yellow pools on the floor, and spoke sharply:

"There's a good spittoon right over there." He exchanged his bundle of papers for others and hastened out again. Bill gently hitched up his trousers, shut his teeth with a snap, and spoke through them with deep feeling.

"That's jist th' way. The fu'ther up in Kansas you go, the more dam p'tickler they git."

Bill Jones was no orator. Like Mark Antony he had "neither wit, nor words nor worth" and yet all unconsciously he had constituted himself the spokesman of a great commonwealth. It was the people of Texas who were speaking through the irregular, tobacco-stained teeth of this lanky cow hand, hinting of a feud hardly less bitter than that of Montague and Capulet. Behind the pungent remark of Bill Jones lay nearly half a century of history, the details of which are now well-nigh forgotten.

Among the pioneer settlers of Kansas the New England element bulked large. The town of Lawrence, together with many other Kansas villages, was founded by New England Puritans. Narrow and bigoted as some of them undoubtedly were, they were nevertheless men who dreamed dreams and saw visions. They had come out to these western prairies, their hearts aflame with one great purpose, the making of Kansas free territory. Descended, moreover, from hardy,

stiff-necked leaders of a church militant, they stood ready
to back their antislavery principles with Sharps rifles. Ideals
were to them something for which men fought. Always they
held in memory the heroic example of an ancestry who had
battled for liberty and made good by force of arms their
declaration that "taxation without representation is tyranny."

Settling upon their 160-acre prairie claims they built rude
sod houses to shelter their families, plowed little fields, and
planted crops. A frugal, industrious, God-fearing people,
they had no fears for the future. They were crusaders called
of God to make Kansas free. Willingly would they endure
privation, heat, cold, drought, hot winds, and the onslaught
of human enemies if only this purpose might be realized.
Ad astra per aspera, the state motto of Kansas, was to them
but a simple statement of the task before them. No matter
how rough and stony the way, they would travel it gladly
if only at the end they might see the stars of freedom shining
above the land they loved and had made their own.

Side by side with the Puritan abolitionists came many other
people. Some were from the prairies of northern Ohio or
Illinois and were New Englanders but two or three generations removed. Others were German immigrants, a thrifty,
pious folk, almost as much opposed to slavery as were the
Puritans themselves. Still others were Scandinavian in origin,
descendants of the old sea kings of northern Europe whose
courage and hardihood have formed the theme of many a
tale and poem. Yet the New England element largely furnished leadership and gave shape and color to the life and
ideals of all the rest.

The people who settled Texas were of a far different
breed. Generally speaking they were southern uplanders,
many of them Scotch-Irish, and were of the most hardy and

adventurous type. Their ancestors had poured westward through Cumberland Gap and other passes of the lower Appalachians to the fertile glades and meadows of Kentucky and Tennessee, pushing a long tongue of settlement far out into the wilderness. Here they had lived in pallisaded stations, or fortress-like log houses, holding with their long rifles these hard-won lands against hordes of painted savages who constantly stormed at the far-flung settlements in a desperate attempt at "letting in the jungle."

Growing up under such conditions, many of their children migrated to Texas to find there ample opportunity for the exercise of those peculiar talents learned in the hard school of life on this older frontier east of the Mississippi. The prowling bands of fierce, treacherous Comanches and the raids of thieving Mexicans made the life of the people of the early Texas settlements one of continuous peril. The rifle, the pistol, and the huge knife named for the Texas pioneer, James Bowie, must be every man's constant companions, and unfortunate indeed was he who lacked skill in the use of them.

Texas was peculiarly a man's country. A woman of this region in early times is credited with having written to relatives in the East that: "Texas is a good country for men and dogs, but an awfully hard place for oxen and women."

Yet there were many women there too; strong, resolute, pioneer women with big, unselfish hearts and busy, skillful hands who shared unflinchingly the hardships and dangers of husband or brother.

Independent and individualist as were the Texans, the ever-present menace of Indian attack forced the people of each settlement into co-operation and mutual helpfulness. This tendency was greatly extended and intensified by the

War of Independence and the years of life under the Republic. A certain solidarity and national consciousness grew up. The people felt themselves cemented together by the blood of Travis and Crockett and Bowie. Common hardships and dangers, plus a remarkable historical heritage, bound them together "with hoops of steel." The Alamo and San Jacinto were to them words quite as sacred as Lexington and Yorktown, and Houston and Austin quite as much national heroes as Washington and Franklin. For ten years they lived under the Lone Star flag, citizens of the independent republic of Texas. Then came annexation to the United States, but the tradition still persisted. Texas had stamped its brand indelibly upon the hearts and lives of its sons and daughters.

Thus by 1860 Texas and Kansas, separated only by the lands of the Indian Territory, had been settled by populations as unlike as any two people can well be. The Texans were a strong, hardy race of men on horseback, proud of themselves and of their state, and of the fact that they had won their broad lands by their might and held them by force of arms against all the power of Mexican and Indian enemies. Proslavery by instinct and training as they were, relatively few of them owned a large number of negroes. Yet they were Southerners. In their blood were the hospitality and the chivalry of the Old South mingled with the hardihood, adventure, and self-reliance of the West.

In so far as they thought of the Kansans at all, it was to regard them as narrow, intolerant, penny-pinching, Yankee abolitionists inhabiting a land where each family was confined to a petty hundred-and-sixty-acre claim, while in their own country every man measured his lands by leagues or square miles. The very qualities which made the people of

Kansas great—thrift, frugality, and a sincere belief in the rights of the poor and ignorant negroes—were in the eyes of the Texans little better than vices and weaknesses. To these men of the Southwest smallness of farms must inevitably connote smallness of ideas, and a willingness to fight for the freedom of the slaves was only wrongheaded obstinacy.

On the other hand the Kansans regarded these men of Texas as a rough, wild, lawless set who rode hard, swore hard, and feared neither God nor man. The hot southern blood and skill in the use of arms branded them in the eyes of the Kansans as dangerous killers, and the latter hinted quite plainly that all too many of the Texans were the descendants of men who had fled beyond the Sabine to escape the penalty for crimes committed elsewhere.

That the Texans were hard riders cannot be denied. Conditions of life in that state often demanded hard riding. This was not due to constant Indian warfare alone, but Texas was by 1860 a great pastoral region. Almost the first Spanish colonists brought in cattle—lean, long-horned animals of the type raised by the Moors for centuries on the plains of Andalusia. These increased amazingly and later mixed with the cattle of north European breeds brought in by the early American settlers. The result was an animal larger and heavier than the early Spanish cattle, yet sufficiently hardy to live and thrive throughout the year upon the open range.

Everything tended to promote the herding industry. The climate was mild, grass and water abundant, and the land laws liberal. Mexico early gave out large land grants to individuals and this policy was continued by the Republic and later by the state of Texas. Huge tracts were sold at low prices upon liberal terms of payment. As a result Texas at the time of the outbreak of the Civil War was, broadly speaking, a region of great land proprietors, many of whom numbered their cattle by hundreds or even by thousands.

The war came and the Texans, "ever ready for a fight or a frolic," and quite likely to regard the fight as a frolic, hastened away to join the armies of Lee, Johnston, or E. Kirby Smith. For four years they fought bravely under the Stars and Bars proving their mettle upon many a blood-stained field. During all this time their homeland was of all states of the Confederacy the least touched by war.

While the army of Sherman ate a hole fifty miles wide across Georgia and the Carolinas, while Virginia was ravaged by armies of both North and South, and while the fields of Louisiana and Mississippi lay fallow and grew up in bushes and briers for want of laborers to till them, the cattle on the broad plains of Texas grew mature and fat and increased rapidly in numbers under the favorable conditions of range and climate. The women and children were able to brand most of the calves each spring, the state was untouched by hostile armies, and the opening of the Mississippi by the North made it impossible for the Confederacy to draw upon the great store of Texas cattle to feed its hungry armies. As a result, when the war closed and the Texans returned to their homes, they found their ranges fairly overflowing with fine, fat cattle.

For these animals there was no market. Stock cattle could be bought upon the range for from one to two dollars a head while a fat beef would sell for not more than six or seven dollars. Yet at this very time cattle were selling upon the northern markets at eight to eleven dollars a hundred pounds, and beef was retailed at from twenty-five to forty cents a pound. Out of this condition grew the so-called "northern drive."

Most of the Texans returning from the southern armies reached home in the summer or early autumn of 1865. An impoverished people, they must look to the only movable property they possessed—the great herds of cattle—for means to support their families and improve their lands. Valueless as these cattle were at home, their owners soon learned of the high price of beef in the northern cities and began to lay their plans to reach a market. Accordingly, in the winter of 1865–66 large herds were collected at many points in Texas preparatory to driving north as soon as grass should be sufficiently advanced to make a start possible.

The journey was usually begun late in March or early in April. The herds varied in size from one thousand to three thousand large choice steers, and each herd was accompanied by the "boss" and from eight to fourteen cowboys, together with a cook who drove the chuck wagon in which the food and bedding were hauled.

The usual route followed was north from central Texas, passing just west of Fort Worth, and traversing the strip of prairie between the upper and lower Cross Timbers, past Denton and Sherman to Red River. Beyond that stream the line of travel was north across the Indian Territory, past Boggy Depot, thence northeast across the two Canadians, and on past Fort Gibson to the Kansas line just south of Baxter Springs.

Skilled as most Texans were in the handling of cattle, and inured as they were to hardship and privation and long days and nights in the saddle, few of them had had much experience in driving great herds for long distances on the trail.

Accounts left by some of these earliest drovers are little better than one long wail of trouble and misery. Heat, cold, hunger, rain, mud, thunderstorms, stampedes, swollen rivers, thieving Indians, outlaw whites, and dissatisfied men are but a few of the troubles complained of by trail bosses on these "personally conducted tours" of the summer of 1866, during the drive from Central Texas to Red River. Once beyond that stream there was added to all these difficulties endless annoyance from the Indians who demanded payment for grass consumed by the cattle, stampeded herds at night in order to collect money for gathering them again, and in many other ways proved themselves a constant source of worry and vexation. The war had but recently closed and conditions within the Indian Territory and along its border were lawless and unsettled. White thieves and outlaws, together with pilfering Indians, stole horses, mules, and cattle and made it necessary for the drovers to watch their property closely at all times.

When they reached the line of Kansas below Baxter Springs, the trail drivers encountered fresh difficulties. Some small herds of Texas cattle had been driven north through Kansas and Missouri just before the war with the result that many native cattle in these two states had died of the dread "Texas fever." In 1866 the settlers of southeastern Kansas had by no means forgotten their losses from this disease in the years just preceding the war. Perhaps the extent of such losses had even been magnified with the passing years as the tale was told and retold about the Kansas firesides. Moreover, the wounds made by the war just closed were still raw and bleeding. To the Kansas abolitionists no good thing could possibly come out of Texas. Least of all could a quarter of a million lean, long-horned, wild, disease-bearing, Spanish steers be considered a blessing. Rather they were a plague infinitely worse than that of the locusts visited upon a stubborn Pharaoh and his people. Armed bands of stalwart Kansas farmers were quickly formed to stop the herds of Texas cattle at the border and to warn the drovers that under no circumstances would they be permitted to advance farther, at least until cold weather should come to eliminate the danger of Texas fever.

This was bitter news to men who for three months had endured every privation and hardship, who had overcome what seemed well-nigh insurmountable obstacles, and had at last reached a point where the worst was clearly over if only they might be permitted to proceed. Nor was such news made sweeter by the fact that it came from the lips of their late victorious antagonists, the "nigger loving Yankee abolitionists" of the North.

The question was complicated by the mysterious and subtle nature of the disease which the Kansans professed to fear—Texas fever. We know now that it is a malady to which southern cattle are entirely immune but which they carry to northern cattle by means of the fever ticks which drop from their bodies and attach themselves to other animals.

The Texans declared that their cattle were perfectly healthy and that it was absurd to suppose that they transmitted disease to others. The Kansans insisted that, absurd or not, when Texas cattle passed near, their own animals sickened and died, and they must assume that these southern cattle brought disease, though they were forced to admit that they did not understand just how or why.

Yet numerous theories were evolved and explanations given. It was asserted by some that a shrub in Texas wounded the feet of cattle making sores from which pus exuded to poison the grass and bring disease to northern animals. Others believed that the breath of Texas cattle upon the grass left

there germs of disease. A few hinted that ticks might have
something to do with the mystery but most people ridiculed
the idea.

However, the Kansas settlers did not concern themselves
much with theories. It was enough that their cattle had died
in the past. It might be a visitation of God or the devil as
a punishment for evil companionship. Certainly they had
no more desire that their cattle associate with Texas longhorns than that they themselves associate with Texas cowpunchers.

Whatever sympathy we may have for the Texas drovers
in their difficult situation, there is nevertheless much to be
said for the attitude of the Kansas settlers. Most of them
were very poor. Some had endured the hardships of life on
a prairie claim for years, others had but recently settled their
homesteads and were striving to maintain themselves in a
new frontier region. Most families had but two or three milk
cows, and the milk and butter supplied by these were the
chief items in the daily bill of fare. If their cattle died it
meant that little children must go hungry or at least suffer
from the lack of proper food. The armed settlers met the
first herds at the border with a fixed determination that they
must be stopped at all hazards. With no less vehemence than
was later shown by the French under far different circumstances they voiced the declaration: "They shall not pass."

The Texans had equal determination but infinitely less
hope of success. They were few in numbers, broken up into
small groups, and far from home and the support of friends
and kindred. Yet they were not men who could be easily
stopped. They thought of their own wives and children for
whom a profitable sale of these cattle meant better food and
clothing and greater comfort. Strong and hardy by nature

and training, they had been made even more so by the trying experiences of the past weeks, during which they had traveled so many weary miles in search of a market for their property. To turn back meant that all their toil and hardship had been in vain. Now that they were comparatively near their goal, they would not relinquish, without a struggle, the enterprise upon which they had embarked.

There were sharp conflicts in some instances, conflicts in which the Texans were foredoomed to failure. Not a few of the drovers were assaulted and beaten and several were killed by Kansas farmers. The cattle were stampeded and driven back into the Indian country. Some few who insisted upon proceeding had their cattle shot down and killed. A writer in the *Prairie Farmer* of August 25, 1866, stated that small herds of Texas cattle had been killed to the last animal by Kansas farmers and that if the owners of such herds insisted upon advancing north, this was the only alternative. He declared that any man who drove Texas cattle into Kansas in warm weather was considered by the border settlers of that state as no better than a horse thief.

Faced by overwhelming odds, some drovers gave up in despair, abandoned their herds, or sold them for anything that might be offered, and rode back to Texas. Others turned their cattle back into the Cherokee Nation to await the coming of cold weather, but prairie fires destroyed much of the grass and it was found very difficult to hold a herd so long in the Indian Territory. A few men turned west through the Cherokee country, and, after driving in that direction until they had passed the western limits of settlement in Kansas, again turned north across that state and a corner of Nebraska to Iowa or, in some cases, to St. Joseph, from which point the animals could be shipped to Chicago.

Some of these men apparently met with a degree of success, but the losses on the trail had been so heavy in most cases as to leave them but a small fraction of the number of animals with which they had left home, and these were usually so thin and weak as to be of little value. Of the 260,000 head of cattle driven north during the summer of 1866 very few ever reached a profitable market.

The Texas cattlemen were almost in despair. There can be little doubt that the returning drovers spread the tale of their mistreatment at the hands of the Kansas settlers until it was known in almost every ranch house and cow camp in the Lone Star State. As a result comparatively few herds were started north in the spring of 1867, and yet that year was to see the solution of the problem of a market for Texas cattle.

This was accomplished largely through the efforts of Joseph G. McCoy, a prominent cattle dealer of Illinois. McCoy was keenly alive to the profits that might be derived from the Texas cattle trade and in the summer of 1867 visited Kansas City. At this time the Kansas Pacific Railway was building westward up the valley of the Kaw and had been constructed as far as Salina, a point far to the west of all settlement. McCoy's plan was to establish a cattle depot, or shipping point, on this railway at some convenient place to the west of any settlements and then urge the Texans to drive their herds to this place and from there ship the animals to Kansas City.

Accordingly he made a journey up this line of railroad and eventually chose as the site of his cattle depot the station of Abilene in Dickinson County. Here he established a town and built great shipping pens and a hotel. He then sent a rider south with instructions to seek out all herds moving north through the Indian Territory and tell the drovers of the shipping facilities afforded by Abilene.

This the rider did, but by this time it was too late to increase the drive from Texas that year, so only the scattered herds already in motion were brought in. Even so, some thirty-five thousand head of Texas cattle were brought to Abilene and shipped to market during that year. The news of the success of these drovers quickly reached Texas and in 1868 the number of cattle driven north increased to seventy-five thousand head. In 1869 it rose to 350,000 head while by 1871 no less than six hundred thousand head of Texas cattle were driven north over the various trails leading from Texas to the cow towns of Kansas.

Abilene was only temporarily the cowboy capital. Within three or four years the homesteaders creeping slowly westward had reached it. McCoy sold out his interests in the town to others who sought to discriminate against the trail drivers and make the former shipping point a market for agricultural products.

The attempt was disastrous. Other lines of railroad were now extending westward through Kansas and new "cow towns" were established upon these, farther west and beyond all settlements. Abilene was virtually deserted and changed from a busy bustling place to a sleepy little village surrounded by a few homesteaders who for some years could sell very little and buy even less.

However, in the course of the transition of Abilene from a cattle market to an agricultural village there were fresh bickerings and misunderstandings between the Texas drovers on one hand and the claim holders and the later owners of the town on the other.

The new cow towns were Wichita, Newton, Ellsworth,

Junction City, Caldwell, and above all, Dodge City. In addition to these were others of minor importance. They were said to be the wickedest towns in all America. To them flocked gamblers, saloon keepers, and the rough, lawless riffraff of the underworld to meet and prey upon the equally rough and lawless Texas cowpunchers who arrived with their summer's wages in their pockets and a thirst accumulated day by day during three or four months travel along the hot and dusty trail.

Dodge City had at one time two graveyards, "Boot Hill," where were buried those men who had died with their boots on, and another on the opposite side of town for those who had died peacefully in bed. The latter cemetery was small and neglected, but "Boot Hill" early had a large and constantly growing population. The first jail at Dodge City was a well fifteen feet deep into which drunks were lowered to remain until they were sober and ready to leave town.

The chief reason for the great prosperity of the Kansas cow towns was that they were half-way points between the great breeding grounds of Texas and the feeding grounds of the northern territories. Within a few years after the close of the Civil War the ranch cattle industry began to spread rapidly over the northern plains. The great reduction of the buffalo herds due to the activities of the hide hunters, coupled with the removal of many Plains tribes of Indians to reservations in Oklahoma and elsewhere, opened up vast new ranges in Colorado, Wyoming, Montana, and Dakota.

Many cattle were driven into all of these territories, and ranches were established wherever there was abundant grass and water. As a result of the opening up of these new ranching areas the drive from Texas to Dodge City frequently was but the first part of a drive to these remote territories.

Enterprising ranchmen from the Northwest came down to Dodge City to purchase cattle to stock their new ranges. To them the Texas trail drivers sold large numbers of young steers while the fat, mature animals were shipped by rail directly to Kansas City or Chicago for slaughter.

An enthusiasm for ranching amounting almost to a craze swept over the entire country. Prominent bankers, lawyers, and statesmen invested money in the business. Young eastern men just out of college, of whom Theodore Roosevelt was a conspicuous example, hastened west to give their personal attention to the ranch cattle industry. The shipments of beef and live cattle to England, Scotland, and the continent of Europe aroused the interest of people in those countries and not a few wealthy foreigners came over and established ranches on the Great Plains. Prominent among these were the Marquis de Mores, a French nobleman, and Baron von Richthofen, grandfather of the noted German ace. Wealthy English and Scottish investors formed syndicates to finance ranching enterprises and the British Parliament sent a commission to this country to investigate and report on the industry.

Texas, because of its warm climate and low altitude, remained the chief breeding ground, while the northern plains, with their cool, bracing atmosphere and rich pasturage lands, became the chief feeding grounds, and not a few men held ranges in both regions.

The enormous number of cattle driven north in the summer of 1871 broke down the market and many men suffered heavy losses. As a result the drive was lessened somewhat, though for the next fifteen years perhaps three to five hundred thousand head were driven north each summer.

The earliest drivers, who sought to break a way across

the western part of Indian Territory and into Kansas far beyond all settlements, experienced some difficulty owing to their lack of knowledge of the route and the fact that there were no trails or well-known landmarks. It was not long, however, until well-defined trails grew up and the route became perfectly familiar.

Trail driving was eventually reduced almost to a science. It was found by "trial and error" methods that about 2,500 head was the correct number for a herd. This number required a trail boss, nine cowboys, a horse wrangler, usually a boy fourteen to sixteen years old, and a cook to drive the chuck wagon. Such a herd moved in a column about a mile in length. The trail boss usually rode ahead to survey the ground and search out watering places and good grazing grounds. Next, at the extreme forward tip of the moving column rode two men, one on either side, called the "point." This was the station of greatest responsibility since it was these two men who must determine the exact direction taken, or "point" the herd. It was here too that a stampede always started. A third of a mile back, where the moving column began to bend in case of a change of course, rode two men, one on either side, at "swing." A third of a mile still farther back rode two men at "flank," while in the rear three men brought up the "drag." The horse wrangler accompanied his *remuda*, or saddle band, of five or six horses for each man. while the chuck wagon usually followed the herd in the morning and preceded it in the afternoon.

Such a herd usually traveled ten or twelve miles a day and could be driven from central Texas to the Canadian border at a total cost of less than a dollar a head, while to ship cattle such a distance by rail at the present time would cost from five to ten times that much.

Indians of the Kiowa-Comanche and Cheyenne-Arapaho reservations in Oklahoma sometimes visited the herds and asked for beef but seldom caused serious trouble. However, the Kansas farmers were slowly but steadily pushing westward. Drovers crossing the line into the state often found a scattering population of homesteaders in a region which the summer before had been entirely without any sign of human habitation. These protested loudly against the advance of the herd, complained of the dangers of Texas fever, and demanded damages for crops injured or destroyed by the cattle. The land-hungry Kansans were advancing toward the setting sun and nothing could stop their progress.

Moved by the growing scarcity of range at home, some of the Texans drove herds into western Kansas and established ranches there, trusting that the great Goddess of Drought would make their tenure of these lands permanent. It was not to be. Within a few years the pioneer settlers began to come among them, build little sod houses, break fields, and sow wheat. Bitter quarrels followed. The homesteaders did not fear disease from the cattle that had been wintered in this region, but they did fear and dislike the owners of these animals. Cattlemen were wicked and unprofitable citizens of an agricultural community—particularly Texas cattlemen. They would never build schools and churches, increase the price of lands, and develop the country. Away with them!

All Texans believed implicitly in the doctrine of "free grass," that is that fields should be fenced and livestock permitted to run at large. The Kansas farmers believed equally strongly in the "herd law," or that livestock should be inclosed and fields left unfenced. Under the Kansas law this question was left for each county to determine for itself.

Eight or ten ranchmen might locate in a county with a million dollars worth of cattle, but the influx of fifty families of homesteaders with property aggregating in value not over twenty-five thousand dollars spelled their ruin. The newcomers homesteaded less than 2 per cent of the land of the county, promptly voted a herd law, and the ranchmen were forced to remove. They went, suffering great financial loss, and with renewed bitterness in their hearts toward the "Kansas Jayhawkers."

In the meantime the fears of the Kansas farmers with regard to fever had been carried to the legislature of that state. Stringent quarantine regulations were enacted against Texas cattle, culminating in the middle eighties with a law prohibiting the bringing of southern cattle into Kansas under any circumstances. This was soon declared to be unconstitutional but a law was passed forbidding the bringing of Texas cattle into Kansas at any time except during the winter months, a season at which it is entirely impossible to move cattle any considerable distance on the trail. The cow towns died instantly, while the Texans swore bitterly and swung their drive far to the west through Colorado, whose quarantine laws were more moderate. Yet some settlers began to occupy the prairies of that state also. In desperation the Texas ranchmen sought relief from Congress and endeavored to have a long strip of the public domain extending from Texas to the Canadian border set aside as a national cattle trail, but their efforts in that direction failed.

In the frightful winter of 1886–87 cattle on the northern plains died by tens of thousands. Many, if not most, of the largest operators in that region were ruined. The severe winter was followed by a period of low prices and the enthusiasm of the country at large with respect to ranching began to cool. The great drives grew smaller and smaller in volume. The length of the drive west through Colorado, the presence of settlers, the fact that the northern plains were now fully stocked, and the surplus of cattle in Texas greatly reduced—all served to reduce the number of cattle sent up the trail each year.

Moreover, trail driving was no longer necessary. Before 1880 the Missouri-Kansas-Texas railway had been completed south from St. Louis to Fort Worth, thus affording a direct line from North Central Texas to market. Seven or eight years later the Santa Fe was completed from Kansas City to Fort Worth, thus giving easy access to the Kansas City markets. Before this time the cause of Texas fever had been discovered and measures taken to prevent the spread of the disease and to effect the ultimate eradication of the fever tick. Quarantine yards were built at all principal markets to which southern cattle intended for slaughter might be shipped and kept entirely separate from others to which they might transmit disease. Also a system of dipping was inaugurated by means of which southern cattle could be cleansed of the dread parasite and so rendered safe from carrying infection.

The drives grew smaller and smaller and by the middle nineties had virtually ceased altogether. Texas cowpuncher and Kansas farmer no longer came together at the border or in the cow towns to impugn one another's motives and ancestry in language far more picturesque and forceful than it was elegant. Each settled back to his own work within his own state free from worry and interference by the other. Yet the years of conflict had done their work. A feud had been created that half a century has not entirely eliminated.

Each told his children of the experiences of earlier days and so kept alive the smoldering spark of disfavor and distrust.

Bill Jones and the thousands of his kind who once moved the vast herds of long-horned cattle northward over the dusty trails are, with few exceptions, no more. "Gone with the things of yesteryear," they have passed, to quote their own language, "up the dim, narrow trail to that new range which never fails, and where quarantine regulations do not exist." Any reasons, or fancied reasons, for hostility between Texas and Kansas have gone with them. Gone, it is true, but unfortunately not yet quite forgotten.

It has been thirty years since the author of this volume called the Lone Star State home, and more than twenty-five years since he has had any financial interest in the ranch cattle business. But once a Texan always a Texan, and once a cowpuncher, always a cowpuncher. The curving legs warped by long years of days and nights in the saddle will straighten themselves sooner than will the curved mind warped during that same period of time. The impressions and prejudices of youth are strong and, like Banquo's ghost, "will not down." So with all respect to my many dear friends of the Sunflower State, I yet feel that there is an element of truth in the words of old Bill Jones:

"The fu'ther up in Kansas you go, th' more dam p'tickler they git."

III

Wagons Hitched to a Star

We pointed the wagon tongue each night
Straight at the old North Star
And started on at the peep of dawn
And tried to travel as far
As the cattle could walk in a single day
And still keep frisky and fat,
Though the days were few when we really knew
Exactly where we were at!
But the boss would say: "We are on our way
And the grass is fresh and green,
So we'll follow that tongue 'till we bust a lung
Or get to Abilene."

THE TRAIL DRIVERS

AS HAS BEEN INDICATED IN THE preceding chapter, the first drovers who started north from Texas with herds of cattle knew comparatively little of trail driving and had neither an exact objective to be reached nor a definite trail to follow. They knew only that somewhere far to the north were markets where cattle might be sold at a price several times greater than they would command in Texas. To reach such a market they were willing to brave all hardships and dangers that might lie in their way. No doubt swollen rivers must be crossed, predatory bands of Indians would be met, and a trail would have to be made as they went. Yet no trail boss who once started with a herd ever turned back. He merely set his wagon each night with the tongue pointing toward the North Star and moved forward the next morning with a fixed determination to make his ten to fifteen miles that day. In a very real sense he "hitched his wagon to a star" and kept his cattle close behind its rolling wheels.

After the founding of Abilene and other cow towns of Kansas, however, it was not long until the route became fairly familiar and definite trails had grown up. The first trail to be used traversed the strip of prairie west of the site of Fort Worth and crossed the Red River into the Indian Territory. From here it continued north across the Choctaw Nation through a hilly, mountainous region into the Cherokee Nation and on north and east past Fort Gibson to a point near Baxter Springs, Kansas, and thence north and a little east into Missouri. West of this lay the West Shawnee Trail, which passed through the Chickasaw Nation and on north past the old Sac and Fox Agency, and so into Kansas.

Still farther west was the famous Chisholm Trail crossing the Red River some miles east of Henrietta, Texas, and continuing north, following approximately the line of the Rock Island railroad which now extends across Oklahoma, past the sites of the present towns of Duncan, Chickasha, El Reno, and Enid and crossing into Kansas near where Caldwell now stands. From here the route led north and east crossing the Arkansas River near the site of the present city of Wichita and on northeast to Abilene.

West of this lay the most famous trail of all, commonly known as the Western Trail. It started far down in Texas near Bandera and ran north past Seymour and Vernon, Texas, crossing the south fork of the Red River near Doan's Store. From there it continued nearly north crossing the North Fork of the Red River into the Kiowa-Comanche reservation and on north across the Cheyenne-Arapaho reservation, crossing the Canadian River a short distance west of the present town of Camargo, and from there continued past Fort Supply to the Kansas border and on to Dodge City.

Even after trails had been definitely established, however, it was not always possible to follow them. Grass might be short in some places or water scarce, or perhaps rumors of acquisitive Indians prompted the trail boss to leave the main trail and cut across to another or to form a new one for himself. In this way "cut offs" and temporary trails were sometimes formed that might either be mistaken for the regular one or that might present to the foreman of a herd the problem of choosing what seemed to be the most advantageous route. This was, however, later after the northern drives had been going on for some time. The early drovers must make their own trails and choose the best route to pursue largely by trial and error methods.

The making up of a herd for the drive north and the assembling of a trail outfit and a suitable crew of men was neither a short nor an easy task. During the earlier years of the drives the Texas ranchman who owned large numbers of cattle chose from his animals a herd of two to three thousand of his oldest and largest steers since the animals were destined to be marketed for slaughter. These were usually five to seven years old and like nearly all of the Texas cattle at this time were the tall, rangy longhorns, often almost as wild as deer and offering no promise of any animal's furnishing either a large quantity or high quality of merchantable beef. To assemble such a herd, it was necessary to hold a roundup and cut out those animals that seemed suitable for driving north to market. This always required several days', and in some cases several weeks', time.

In the meantime while the beef herd was being formed it was necessary to make ready an outfit for the long drive which was certain to last for three or four months. This must include a large covered wagon drawn by four mules, to carry the food, bedding, and camp equipment. The canvas cover was spread over five or six hickory bows, fitted into sockets on the outside of the wagon box and drawn tight so as to protect the contents from rain. A chuck box

was constructed which fitted exactly into the rear of the
wagon box when the endgate had been removed. This was
about four feet tall and was held in place by the wagon rods
which ordinarily held the rear endgate of the wagon box
in place. The chuck box was about eighteen inches or two
feet deep from front to rear at the bottom, but the sides
were sloped upward so that it was not more than six inches
deep at the top. It was fitted with shelves which were in
turn divided into compartments by partitions. The deeper
compartments at the bottom held the "sour dough jar,"
flour, and other bulky groceries, while the middle ones, not
so deep, contained sugar, rice, beans, coffee, and syrup, and
the small upper ones tin cans of soda, baking powder, salt,
pepper, and other articles used from day to day in cooking.
The rear wall of the chuck box was hinged at the bottom
and was fitted with a hinged leg at the middle of the upper
edge so it could be lowered, forming a table at which the
cook could work while preparing a meal. It is doubtful if
any better form of camp kitchen has ever been devised than
was the chuck box at the rear of a trail driver's wagon.

The bulk of the food supply was, of course, carried in the
wagon box. A ten-gallon keg for water was attached to the
side of the wagon, and the heavy Dutch ovens, pots, and
other cooking utensils were carried on a rack built beneath
it. With a wagon thus equipped, it remained only for the
drover to purchase supplies for the journey and to employ
a cook, horse wrangler, and a sufficient number of men to
handle the herd.

Few records have come down to us concerning the provisions carried by the wagons of the very early trail drivers.
Probably they consisted largely of corn meal, coffee, beans,
molasses, and perhaps a few sides of bacon, though for a

meat supply they probably depended upon slaughtering a beef every few days. For the drives made in the late seventies and eighties, however, we have better records, since the account books of many merchants supplying trail herds are still in existence.

A dozen men require a great deal of food for a journey lasting three to six months and while the supply could be replenished from time to time after occasional stores had been established along the trail, these were never numerous and for a long time were indeed few and far between. In consequence, it was necessary for the boss to see to it that his wagon was well provisioned when the drive began. Flour, beans, coffee, sugar, salt, syrup or molasses, bacon, and dried fruit were, of course, staples. To these must be added soda and baking powder, and often rice commonly known as "moonshine." Some outfits that were noted for generosity in the matter of feeding their men would add, during the later years of the drives, onions and a keg of pickles, and in some instances a few cases of canned tomatoes or corn. Roasted coffee was usually purchased in the bean and the cook ground a supply for each meal in a coffee mill screwed to the side of the chuck box.

In the case of the very earliest drives, the owner of the cattle usually went along and was his own trail boss, but as the business grew in magnitude many great ranchmen in Texas would send several herds north in a single season. This, of course, made it necessary to employ a foreman or trail boss for each herd. He was always an able and experienced man in whose resourcefulness and good judgment the owner had ample confidence. He was usually paid about $125 a month and his responsibility was very great since to him was entrusted not only property that might be worth

$100,000 or more, but also the welfare and safety of the men. In the sense that his authority was supreme he was like the captain of a ship, but there the similarity ended. The men respected his authority and sought diligently to carry out his orders, but in all other respects he was one of them. They called him by his first name in most cases, and he, of course, ate the same food they did, slept in the same type of bed, and did not in any sense hold himself aloof from the humblest rider.

Next to the foreman the cook was the most important man with the herd. He usually received five or ten dollars a month more than the riders and probably earned it. He must get up an hour before daylight each morning in order to have breakfast ready by dawn, must wash and store away the dishes three times a day, prepare food that was satisfying, and must in addition be able to drive and handle four temperamental mules. It is true that the men helped out a bit whenever possible. They would drag up wood with a rope at night for the breakfast fire and often assist at other small tasks around camp. Often the cook was something of an autocrat or at least stood firmly upon his traditional rights, demanding that every man, from the boss to the wrangler, roll up his bedding and tie it into a neat bundle each morning so that it was ready for loading. Nevertheless, he kept the food and coffee hot for latecomers, tried to vary the menu as much as possible, and did his best to prepare tasty grub three times a day. A good camp cook was a treasure worthy of admiration and respect, which he usually received in full store.

The humblest individual in a trail outfit was the horse wrangler, usually a boy anywhere upwards of fourteen years of age. From five to ten horses must be provided for each rider, which made a sizable band of forty-five to eighty or ninety head. It was the wrangler's duty to round up the horses each morning and drive them into an impromptu corral made by stretching ropes from each end of the wagon so that every rider could catch his mount required for the day. This must also be done at noon if it were necessary to change horses in the middle of the day, but if things were going smoothly the same horse might be ridden all day. The saddle band must again be driven up in the evening, however, to enable each man to catch and saddle his "night horse" to ride while standing night guard or in case of a stampede. The band of horses was variously known as the *remuda*, "saddle band," or the *caballada*, sometimes corrupted into "cavvy yard," "cavalry yard," or "cavvy." The horse wrangler, if only a lad, was often subject to a certain amount of good-natured chaffing and occasional practical jokes, but his youthful vagaries were usually treated with kindly tolerance by the men who, in most cases, showed for him a rough solicitude closely akin to affection. He was, after all, only a kid to be cared for a bit; a cow hand in embryo; a page or squire who had not yet won his spurs but was on the way!

For a trail herd of upwards of two thousand head, it was necessary to employ at least eight riders in addition to the foreman, and an extra one was often added in case someone should be hurt or become ill. Naturally it was desirable that these be able, experienced, and resourceful men but since "top hands" were never too plentiful this was in all probability too much to expect. In any case, however, at least three or four must be first-class cow hands and the remainder men who had had at least a reasonable amount of experience. Each rider provided his own saddle, slicker, and bedroll, and sometimes brought a horse which was thrown into the *remuda* for his personal use apart from work. If the boss were short of horses and a rider brought an individual horse to be used as a part of his regular mount, he might be given a slight increase in wages.

Often the owner of a trail herd had "made it up" by adding to his own cattle many animals purchased from other ranchmen. In such a case they of course bore different brands, and even if the herd consisted entirely of cattle that he had owned for some time the brands might vary since every large ranchman usually owned cattle of at least two or three brands. This made it necessary that the animals be "road branded" before starting, which was accomplished by running them through a chute and branding them lightly with a bar or slash on the side, shoulder, or hip.

When all of this preliminary work had been completed a day was set for the start. This was usually early in April, or at any rate as soon as grass "had risen" sufficiently to furnish abundant pasturage. Fortunate was the trail boss who had been able to secure a crew of competent and trusty men, and unfortunate was the one who found himself dependent upon the services of a group of worthless "saddle bums."

In 1607 Captain John Smith at Jamestown fervently declared that he wished he "had some real men" instead of the kind which he had there. In the late nineties the author accompanied a trail boss from Oklahoma to northern Texas to receive a herd of a thousand steers that had been purchased for delivery on October first. Since they were to be driven north to a range less than 250 miles away, the foreman took with him, in addition to the author, only a cook driving the chuck wagon and a wrangler with the saddle band of horses, depending upon hiring half a dozen men at the little town where the cattle were to be received. This proved a difficult task. All that could be had were five or six pool hall loafers who claimed that they had once been cow hands, and with these a start was made. At the end of the first day the boss voiced the exact words used by the famous captain at Jamestown nearly three hundred years before. He said: "I wish I had some real men, instead of the kind we've got here!" Truly history repeats in the carrying out of any venturesome enterprise "which has a stomach in it."

The first few days of driving a trail herd constituted a critical period for the foreman. Not only must he get the measure of his men but the cattle were not yet "road broke" and had to be handled with care and real skill. Some trail bosses thought it best to push the herd hard for the first few days on the theory that they would thus become accustomed to the serious business of travel, but more important would be so tired at night that they would be content to lie down and rest until morning. Others felt that harrying the cattle and driving them too hard at first merely tended to make them nervous and unmanageable and preferred gentle treatment, a leisurely start, and getting the herd gradually accustomed to the trail.

In any case, however, the utmost care was taken to avoid a stampede and if one occurred to check it as soon as possible. Stampeding at night seemed to be a habit-forming practice. After two or three had occurred in close sequence, the cattle became highly nervous and difficult to handle and were likely to stampede again upon the slightest provocation. A clap of thunder, the approach of a prowling coyote, the rustling of a slicker, or any other unexpected noise, was sufficient to bring them to their feet like a flash and send the whole herd off in mad flight, their thundering hoofs and crashing horns creating a roar not unlike that of a violent tempest.

After the first few days if the herd did not develop any unmanageable tendencies, the drive settled down to a more or less steady routine and yet eternal vigilance was always necessary, while even the best administered and least exciting trip up the trail was not without its interest as well as hardship and adventure. The cook arose an hour before dawn, kindled a fire, and began the preparation of breakfast. Coffee was put to boil in a huge tin pot with a wide base so that it could not be easily overturned. A batch of sour-dough biscuits was made and baked in one or two large Dutch ovens, and beef steak or bacon fried in a huge, long-handled skillet. Syrup and dried fruit, which had been cooked the night before, were set out together with sugar in a tin can. The dishes and utensils used were tin plates, cups, and spoons, together with knives and forks with handles of wood, bone, or iron. When breakfast was about ready the cook called the men in a loud voice: "Hey! Roll out, you waddies! Here's another day, and grub's ready. Come and get it 'fore I throw it in the creek."

With yawns, groans, and profane ejaculations the men would roll from between their blankets and reach for whatever articles of clothing they had removed before going to bed. In warm weather, if there was little fear of a stampede, the men would strip to their underwear, but if the night were chilly, might remove only their boots and belts, loosen their shirt collars, and lie down otherwise fully dressed.

In any case, dressing was a short and simple matter. Then a hasty wash in a tin pan of cold water, and a drying of the hands and face on a community towel. After this was finished each dragged a pocket comb a few times through his hair and then seized a tin plate and loaded it with hot biscuits, steak or bacon, syrup, commonly known as "lick," and dried peaches or apples. A breakfast like this washed down by a couple of cups of scalding hot coffee put a man in shape to face the day's work.

By the time the men had finished eating the wrangler had driven up the horses and while these were held in the improvised rope corral, each man caught and saddled the mount he wanted, transferring his saddle from the "night horse" staked near the wagon. They then rode out to the herd, which was by this time up and grazing, in order to relieve the two men of the last night-herding shift and let them come in for breakfast and to change their own horses for fresh ones.

The cattle were allowed to graze for a little while and were then drifted off slowly toward the north, grazing as they went. By about nine o'clock the hunger of the animals was reasonably satisfied and they had been strung out into a moving column perhaps nearly a mile in length. The two men riding at "point" directed the herd, while the four men riding at "swing" and "flank" kept the moving column properly strung out and checked the tendency of any animals to straggle. In the rear two or three men at "drag" urged on the lazy, sluggish animals or any that were weak or footsore. The foreman usually rode on some distance ahead of the herd to survey the route, be sure that the road was passable for the wagon, and to see that the leaders did not approach too close to some other herd in advance of his own since a mix-up entailed endless grief and hard riding in order to separate the two herds again. He was likely to be almost anywhere, however, since it was necessary at times to give instructions and to see that everything ran smoothly and in orderly fashion. The wrangler looked after the horses that usually trailed along beside the cattle.

In the meantime the cook had washed the dishes, loaded the bedrolls and camp equipment into the wagon, and hitched up the mules. While the cattle were still grazing he pulled out past the herd and drove five to seven miles to a spot designated by the boss on a stream where there would be abundant water for the cattle. Here he unhitched and staked or hobbled the mules, collected wood for a fire, and began the preparation of dinner. By about twelve o'clock the herd had arrived and the cattle were spread out up and down the stream where they might graze and drink.

After all the men had eaten the cook again washed up the dishes and moved out with the wagon to another designated spot near a stream where he encamped the wagon and began the preparation of supper. After beans or a large piece of beef had been put on the fire to boil, he usually had a couple of hours or more of leisure. Sometimes if the stream showed what looked like some good fishing holes, he would bring out a hook and line, cut a dogwood or willow pole, and catch a mess of fish to vary the monotony of camp fare. At other times he might take a gun and wander along the stream to shoot a turkey or two or half a dozen squirrels, or would pick a bucket full of wild blackberries, dewberries, or sand-hill plums to make a cobbler as a special delicacy to please the men. More often perhaps he would merely spread a blanket in the shade of the wagon and lie down to "catch up on his sleep," rising once in a while to replenish the fire and so keep the pot simmering.

In the meantime, the herd had been "held on the water"

for two or three hours and was then drifted off slowly to the north usually reaching the wagon while the sun was still an hour or more high. The cattle were again "thrown upon the water" under the guard of two or three riders, while the remaining men ate supper and changed mounts. They then relieved the others so that they might come in and eat. Toward sundown the herd was moved out away from the stream to a stretch of level land which would furnish a suitable "bed ground."

Here as twilight fell over the plains the cattle began to lie down and within a few minutes the entire herd was at rest, the animals contentedly chewing their cuds since they were full of grass and water and "decently tired" from the day's drive. The two riders forming the first shift of night guard now took up their task of circling slowly about the herd often singing hoarsely the old cowboy songs—"Bury Me not on the Lone Prairie," "Get Along Little Dogies," or "The Dying Cowboy." It was believed that the voice of the singing riders helped to reassure the animals and keep them quiet and made it less likely that some sudden, unexpected noise would start a stampede.

The first guard usually rode until eleven o'clock, judging the time, if there was no watch in camp, by the moon or by the Great Dipper circling about the North Star. Then one man rode in to wake up the next guard who came out promptly and rode until two in the morning. The cattle would usually get up at midnight to stretch themselves and walk about a little. Any tendency to keep on walking and grazing was promptly checked and within a few minutes they would all lie down again and rest until dawn. At two o'clock the last shift was awakened and came out to take over the task of riding night herd until daylight. The two men of the middle watch returned to the wagon to resume their interrupted sleep until at the first peep of dawn the entire crew was routed out by the booming voice of the cook announcing the coming of another day and breakfast.

Men varied shifts from time to time since the first was regarded as best and the middle one was usually considered the worst. Also with eight or nine riders and only two for each watch every man was able to get a full night's sleep a couple of times a week unless a stampede or other troubles came to break the routine and, in some cases, keep all hands in the saddle the entire night.

By the foregoing it will be seen that a day on the trail involved long hours in the saddle but might otherwise not be particularly hard if the weather were fine and the cattle tractable. Unfortunately such was not always the case. Heavy rains sometimes made the trail almost impassable for the wagon and turned every creek and river into a raging torrent. At such times life was trying. The riders trailed along with the herd, the rain beating against their long, yellow slickers and pouring off their wide-brimmed hats. The cook did his best but it was difficult to start a fire and keep it going with wet wood so the food sometimes had to be served soggy and half raw. If the wagon stuck in the mud it had to be pulled out again by means of ropes tied to the saddle horns. If a wide, swollen river were reached with water too deep to be forded, it was necessary to cut two large cottonwood logs and lash one to either side of the wagon so that it would not sink. It was then "floated across" by towing it over by two or three riders pulling it with their ropes attached to the horns of their saddles.

The herd could be swum across but at times it was difficult to induce the leaders to enter the water. This was usually accomplished by one man riding ahead and in a sense showing the way, but in some cases the stubborn animals steadfastly refused to follow in spite of harrying and urging with the result that a whole day or more would be consumed in fording a stream.

If the river were wide and deep the danger to both men and animals might be considerable. A horse in some cases either could not or would not swim and the rider must slip from the saddle and reach shore as best he could. If he were a poor swimmer or should become entangled in his rope or the floating branch of a tree, he might easily drown. The leading cattle upon reaching the middle of the stream would sometimes attempt to turn back. Those behind them would follow and a "mill" would be established in which the animals would swim around and around in a circle until they drowned unless it were quickly broken up and the leaders again headed for the opposite shore.

On rainy nights it was possible for the men to keep reasonably dry, for the bedroll usually consisted of three or four blankets and a long piece of heavy, nearly waterproof, canvas or tarpaulin. The blankets were spread on one end of this and it was then pulled over them and if necessary over the sleepers' heads. There were sometimes attached to the sides of this snaps and rings which could be utilized in holding the edges together and keeping out wind and rain.

If a stampede started at night the first sound of the running cattle brought every man out of bed in an instant to leap into the saddle on his "night horse" picketed near by and dash madly away through the inky blackness in an effort to reach and turn the leaders. Once this was done and a "mill" established, all hands rode rapidly around the milling herd to prevent their again getting started in a run across the prairie. Eventually the cattle might stop, grow quiet, and lie down again, but sometimes they continued to circle about for hours, keeping all hands riding hard until daylight.

On some rainy evenings when the air was heavily charged with electricity the cattle seemed to be possessed of a legion of devils. Nervous and restive, they would refuse to lie down and kept every rider up all night in order to prevent their stampeding.

Once across Red River the trail drivers were in the Indian Territory and here came new complications. Both the Western and Chisholm trails passed through the lands of the Cheyenne-Arapaho Indians, and the former also crossed the Kiowa-Comanche reservation, while the latter skirted closely its eastern border. Except during the first few years of trail driving these Indians were never hostile, but since the cattle were driven across their lands and consumed their grass they felt, quite justly perhaps, that they were entitled to some compensation in the form of beef. Once in the Indian country every herd was subject to frequent visits from painted warriors with demands for one or more beeves.

Almost every foreman was willing to be reasonable, for if he refused the demand there was grave danger that the Indians would return at night and stampede and scatter the herd, thereby causing great trouble and vexatious delays. Moreover, in reassembling the cattle he would be fortunate if at least three or four were not left behind, upon which the red men and their families would feast once the herd was again well on its way. Yet it was more than two hundred miles across the Indian Territory and if the foreman were too generous in dealing with these tribesmen, he was certain to reach the Kansas border with his herd considerably depleted. This was especially true since the "moccasin telegraph" was remarkably efficient and any group of Indians who found their demands fully met would be certain to pass information on to their brethren farther up the trail that a kindhearted trail boss was coming their way with a herd and that they had better watch for him.

Accordingly the boss usually discounted their requests very considerably, offering to give two or three beeves instead of the six or eight requested. These were at first any lump jaws, or lame animals since the Indians were by no means particular, but long before the Indian country had been crossed such unmerchantable cattle were all gone from the herd and any beeves given to the Indians must be sound animals.

If two or three head of cattle happened to be lost from a herd, it was always customary for the next outfit that came along to pick them up and either turn them over to the owner at the end of the drive or sell them and pay him the money. A foreman who was crossing the Cheyenne country once picked up a fine, fat steer belonging to a herd two or three days drive in advance. A few days later he was visited by an old Cheyenne chief bearing a note from the owner of the advance herd which read: "This is a good old Indian. Give him a beef and he will not trouble you." The boss promptly ordered the boys to cut out this particular steer and give him to the Indian and later joked the owner unmercifully about how promptly his request had been carried out.

Another trail boss received a visit from an old Kiowa chief who demanded six beeves. "I'll give you two but not six," was the answer. "Two not enough," said the old Kiowa haughtily. "You give me six or I'll come with my young men tonight and stampede your cattle." "Well," replied the boss, "when you come tonight be sure to bring a spade with you."

"Why spade?" asked the chief.

"Well," said the foreman, "the cook broke the handle out of our spade yesterday, and when you come to stampede my cattle I aim to kill you and unless you bring a spade along we can't bury you."

The old chief decided to take the two beeves and be satisfied with them.

Occasionally an enterprising foreman was able to come out ahead in his dealings with the Indians. At least a contemporary writer relates that one trail boss who was visited by a band of Cheyennes yielded to their demands for five beeves and then won them all back and ten Indian ponies besides on a horse race!

Pasturing cattle on the Indian reservations was for many years forbidden by the Department of the Interior, except in the case of the herd of an occasional beef contractor held on the range near the agency. In consequence, the grass, except along the trails where it had been cropped close by passing herds, grew rank and luxuriant often tempting a foreman to turn aside and pasture his herd for several days, sometimes a number of miles from the trail. The cattle could thus be rested and recruited to such a point that every animal had gained very considerably in weight. Usually, however, within two or three weeks the outfit would be visited by the Indian agent and several of his Indian police angrily demanding that the trail boss move his cattle on.

During their stay, however, life was leisurely and in most cases very pleasant. A couple of men could easily "day herd" the cattle, and the remainder of the crew were free to fish, hunt, gather wild fruit in the summer or pecans in the autumn, or merely rest, play cards, and enjoy life as best they could.

"Come on boys," called the boss to the author and his companions when during an autumn drive a ten-day stop had been made on the Comanche reservation. "Let's go down there and frail some of them big pecans off that tree."

As a matter of fact the chief diversion of the men during this entire interlude was gathering pecans and the drive was resumed with many bushels of the toothsome nuts stored away in the wagon. During the remainder of the drive the location of the "bed ground" could almost be traced each morning by the pecan shells on the prairie about its outer border since the night herders ate pecans all night long cracking them on the saddle horn with a pocket knife as the riders circled slowly about the sleeping herd.

A stop for ten days or so on one of the Indian reservations or in the Cherokee Outlet was in the nature of a real vacation for both men and beasts. The horses rested and grew fat and frisky, the cattle steadily increased in flesh, and the cook with more abundant leisure prepared excellent food of wider variety than he could ordinarily serve on the trail. A fat beef was slaughtered and the carcass hung to the branch of a tree near the wagon providing delicious roasts, boiled beef with drop dumplings, and barbecued ribs. The men with time to spare would also forage for fresh delicacies. Strings of fish were brought in to be fried for supper, a fat deer or a few turkeys made a welcome change from beef and bacon, or a pot of wild greens might be gathered and boiled. Early in the season it might be possible to find a wild turkey's nest giving the unexpected treat of eggs for breakfast and in rare cases a bee tree might be found and cut and several pails of honey brought to camp. After such a period of rest and recreation the drive was always resumed with everyone in high spirits and a willingness to meet and overcome any obstacles that might lie ahead.

The southern border of Kansas was crossed on the two western trails far to the west of all settlements of homesteaders and so the troubles which had proved so disastrous to the earliest drivers were avoided. Once Dodge City, Abilene, Newton, or whichever cow town had been selected as a destination, had been reached, the herd was held on the prairie a few miles away, while the boss rode in to town and made arrangements to secure cars for shipping the animals to market, or arranged a sale to a broker who shipped them himself. This was true only if the herd was composed of fat, mature steers destined for immediate slaughter.

As ranching began to spread over the northern plains, however, the Kansas cow towns became very important markets for young steers to be used to stock these northern ranges. In fact, after 1880 by far the greater number of herds driven north were made up of steers two years old or younger to be sold to northern ranchmen for maturing on the rich pasturage to be found within the limits of the present states of Wyoming, Montana, and the Dakotas.

Ranchmen who had established headquarters on a range in this region would often come down to Dodge City or some other trail town in order to buy cattle to stock it. Sometimes he would bring a complete crew of men with which to move the cattle on up the trail. Since this, however, would involve the payment of wages for a considerable length of time during which the men were entirely idle, he often brought only a cook with the chuck wagon, a *remuda*, and horse wrangler and depended upon hiring enough men to move the cattle north to his ranch, while he either acted as his own trail boss or employed one if circumstances required his returning home at once.

If the herd were made up of young steers and was sold to a northern ranchman who had brought with him only his chuck wagon and *remuda*, he often hired the entire crew of riders to continue the drive to Dakota or Montana, while the boss, the cook with the wagon, and the wrangler and horses promptly set out on the return journey to Texas. Under such circumstances the drive to the Kansas cow town was for the other men only the first half of a far longer drive which might extend nearly to the Canadian border. Naturally two or three men might decide that they had had enough of trail driving for the present and would refuse further employment and elect to return with the boss to Texas.

On the other hand if the herd were composed of fat, mature cattle to be shipped to market for slaughter, the responsibility of the boss and his men ended when the animals had been sold to a shipper and loaded on the cars. If the boss had orders to ship them himself, cars were secured and he and most, if not all, of the men accompanied them to Kansas City in order to care for the cattle during the journey and effect a sale at its end. They then returned to pick up the wagon, wrangler, and *remuda* and started on the long ride back to Texas.

As the range cattle industry continued to spread over the northern plains, many Texas ranchmen discovered that it was advantageous to secure a range in the north for maturing animals bred in Texas and retained there until they were about two years old. The Texas ranch then became primarily a breeding range and from it were sent herds of these young steers to be matured and fattened for market in the cool, bracing, northern climate where the animals grew larger and heavier than they did under the warm, sunny skies of the Lone Star State. Such a drive must be started early in the spring and, since ten or fifteen miles a day is about as far as a trail herd can be expected to travel, often did not end until the growing chill of autumn nights warned that winter was fast coming. On such a drive the herd was often not taken through Kansas at all but was swung west near the northern border of Indian Territory and driven north through eastern Colorado. This route not only afforded better pasturage by keeping out of the area heavily grazed by herds destined for the cow towns but also avoided the Kansas quarantine regulations which that state later imposed upon Texas cattle to the great vexation of all southern ranchmen.

Any man who made his first long drive from Texas to Montana or Dakota was likely to feel at its end that the experience had given him something in the nature of a liberal education, at least of sorts. The hardships and dangers met due to storms, stampedes, and swollen rivers, the problems he had helped to solve, and the many examples of fortitude and sheer nerve which he had witnessed had all served to make of him a changed man. Certainly he could thereafter always qualify as a "top hand."

Perhaps trail driving could hardly be classed as an extra-hazardous occupation and yet many men were hurt and not a few killed on the trail. If a man were hurt by a fall from a horse or some other cause, the boss and one or two of the "old hands" cared for him as best they could. Many a trail boss or "top hand" showed considerable aptitude for a rough form of surgery and could pull a dislocated shoulder back into place or set a broken arm or leg with considerable skill, using willow sticks or pieces of a grocery box for splints. The injured man was then loaded into the wagon and made as comfortable as possible until he was again able to ride or, if too badly hurt, until he could be taken to some place where he might receive medical attention. Fortunately wounds healed quickly because of the clear, pure air of the plains, and the native strength and hardihood of most of these men usually pulled them through any but the most serious of injuries without too much difficulty or inconvenience. Yet, the pronounced limp of not a few old cow hands gave mute testimony to the improvised surgical treatment which they had received at some time in the past.

If a man were killed during a drive the boss gave him as nearly a Christian burial as was possible under the circumstances. A grave was dug beside the trail and the body properly dressed was carefully, and even tenderly, wrapped in a blanket. A canvas tarpaulin or wagon sheet was then wrapped about it as an outer covering and neatly and firmly tied with ropes. As the men stood by with uncovered heads the body was lowered into the grave and the foreman said a few appropriate words or read a brief passage from a soiled and tattered Testament. After the grave had been filled and the mound neatly rounded up, a bit of board was set up at the head on which was placed the name and date. But the drive, as the actors say of the show, "must go on." The cook had, as ever, set the nearby wagon with the tongue pointing toward the North Star, and the next morning the herd was moved out with the sobered and saddened men casting an occasional glance backward to the little mound which marked the last resting place of a cow hand who in the line of duty had crossed the Great Divide "to that new range which never fails."

It has been estimated that more than five million head of cattle were driven north from Texas during the twenty-year period from 1866 to 1885. The drive then began to decline but continued at least in some measure for a decade longer. This was a movement of great significance in the economic history of our country. Trails running north and south were established, cutting across the earlier established lines of travel and transportation which virtually always ran east and west. The Southwest was brought into contact with the Northwest and the trails along which flowed such vast streams of cattle were the forerunners of trunk lines of railway which were extended from the North to the Southwest mainly in order to give the Texas ranchmen a quicker and easier means of reaching markets with their cattle.

Not only were vast numbers of fat, mature cattle driven northward over the trail to be marketed for slaughter, but an even greater volume of young animals to stock new ranges on the northern plains. This served to reduce the price of beef in eastern towns and cities in the years immediately following the Civil War when the stocks of cattle had been so greatly depleted in the North and East by the years of conflict. Most important of all, this great flood of young cattle which flowed north out of Texas was soon spread out over the central and northern plains area, and within a few years brought into being that great empire of grass, called the Cow Country.

Part III

The Development of the Cow Country

IV

An Empire of Grass

Our empire stretched from Canada
To far off Mexico
And all of us who loved it
Had proudly seen it grow.
We thought it was eternal
With foundations firm and strong,
And no simple "kaffir corner"
Could convince us we were wrong.
How short is human vision!
How soon we saw it pass!
For our empire quickly crumbled;
We had builded it on grass.

AN EMPIRE OF GRASS

THE GREAT STREAM OF TEXAS CATTLE which poured north in the years immediately following the close of the Civil War consisted largely of fat, mature animals destined for immediate slaughter. As the possibilities of ranching on the central and northern plains became apparent, however, most herds began to be made up largely of young steers with which to stock these northern ranges. Of 164 herds aggregating 384,000 head that were driven north in the summer of 1881 about 242,000 head or nearly two-thirds were yearlings and two-year-old steers while the remainder consisted of three- and four-year-old steers and cows. These young steers were sold to northern cattlemen to be matured for two or three years more on the rich pasture lands of their newly established ranches.

Young men lured by the promise of huge profits were eagerly establishing such ranches on every part of the central and northern plains area where abundant grass and water could be found, and these largely looked to Texas, the cradle of the range cattle industry, for animals to stock their newly acquired ranches. In the decade from 1870 to 1880 the number of cattle in Kansas increased in round numbers from 374,000 to 1,534,000; in Nebraska from 80,000 to 1,174,000;

Colorado, 70,000 to 790,000; Montana, 37,000 to 428,000; Wyoming, 11,000 to 521,000; and Dakota, 12,000 to 141,000. Even after due allowances are made for errors or discrepancies in census returns these figures are startling and reveal clearly what was taking place on the Great Plains. A vast pastoral empire was being rapidly created there—an empire of grass which did not reach its greatest size or the zenith of its power and importance until half a dozen years later. Before the end of this six-year period from 1880 to 1886 there can be no doubt that the number of cattle in all of the states indicated, particularly the last three named, had been vastly increased.

In extent of territory this was truly an empire. It stretched from the southern point of Texas to the Canadian border, a distance of some sixteen hundred miles or approximately that from London to Moscow, and its width, to the base of the Rockies, averaged from four hundred to six hundred miles. Beyond the first chain of mountains lay long valleys and still farther west were the deserts, or semideserts, of the Great Basin and of New Mexico and Arizona areas, actually a part of the Cow Country but with a separate history outside the scope of this study, which is concerned primarily with the so-called "short grass country," or Great Plains. Like every pastoral region it was sparsely populated and the society primitive and rough. Its economic basis was grass and the animals which consumed this, so it can in truth be called an "empire of grass."

Title to comparatively little of the soil of this huge empire was vested in private individuals. Outside of Texas the greater part of the land was part of the public domain of the United States, though alternate sections of broad strips extending across the plains had been given to the transcontinental railways. Large areas in Dakota, Montana, and Wyoming had been, as already indicated, set aside for Indian reservations, while almost the entire western half of the present state of Oklahoma, a region approximately as large as the state of Ohio, had been assigned to various tribes of Indians. All of these Indians and the reservations occupied by them were under the direct control of the Indian Bureau of the Department of the Interior, which forbade white intrusion upon such lands, though cattlemen eventually began to pasture herds there under permission granted by the tribesmen themselves. The railroads were in most cases holding their lands until such time as they could be sold profitably to actual settlers and in the meantime interposed little objection to their use by ranchmen for pasturage, though in some cases a small fee was paid for this privilege.

The public domain, after the passage of the homestead act of 1862, was open to entry by homesteaders, but for many years few qualified homesteaders took advantage of this opportunity. Agricultural settlement which had moved steadily westward ever since the time of earliest colonization hesitated upon reaching the edge of these wide, treeless plains, reluctant to attempt to deal with a region so different from that to which it had been accustomed. True, the time was to come when the homesteaders were to pour westward in an ever increasing flood, at first undermining and eventually overwhelming completely the great pastoral empire which was the Cow Country, but that was later. For some years the range riders were left in comparatively undisturbed possession of the region which they had made their own.

Within the limits of Texas the status of the land was somewhat different. The Lone Star State when admitted to the Union had retained possession of its own unoccupied lands as a state public domain. It, too, soon made large grants to railroads, usually in alternate sections, and other large areas were set aside for the use of the public schools. Also both in Texas and New Mexico there was the added complication that numbers of large individual grants had been made by the kingdom of Spain, the Republic of Mexico, or the Republic of Texas, during the various stages of the state's checkered and colorful history. Because of such grants occasional large tracts might be in private hands but on the whole much of the pasture land of Texas was like that of similar lands beyond its borders—public domain—the only difference being that the title was vested in the state and not in the nation. This meant, however, that the laws regarding the disposition of this public domain were made by the Texas legislature rather than by Congress, and Texas was far more liberal in its land policies than was the national government. In consequence it was comparatively easy to secure title in fee to large bodies of Texas land and as a result ranches in that state were often very large and the cattle industry was on a more stable basis than when carried on in the precarious fashion incident to pasturing the public domain of the United States or Indian reservations. The officials of the Texas government, moreover, had a far better understanding of the range cattle business than did Congress and dealt with its problems in a more sane and sympathetic fashion than did the latter body.

But the temporary and uncertain nature of land tenure on the central and northern plains did not prevent the rapid spread of ranching in that region. As the buffalo disappeared from the prairies and the Indians were rounded up and placed on reservations, cattle began to cover these ranges in ever increasing numbers.

As a matter of fact a few men had engaged in cattle raising in this region even before the outbreak of the Civil War. In 1859, J. W. Iliff had gone to Colorado with the gold seekers and failing to find gold had removed to a point near the present town of Laramie where he established a little store and eventually accumulated a small herd of cattle by purchasing poor, lame, and footsore animals from emigrants on the trail to California. This herd grew in time to large proportions and Iliff began to supply beef to the construction camps of the Union Pacific railway. It was not many years before he became one of the best-known ranchmen in Colorado and Wyoming.

Colonel J. D. Henderson, another of the Pike's Peak gold seekers also established a store on the California trail and assembled a considerable herd by the purchase of lame and footsore cattle from the emigrants. His store was located on an island in the Platte River and was a well-known stopping place for caravans journeying westward. After the drives north from Texas began, both Iliff and Henderson added to their herds by purchasing large numbers of these Texas cattle, each eventually coming to own many thousand head. Edward Creighton, of Omaha, Nebraska, also began grazing cattle in that region as early as 1859, as did a few other men.

All of these, however, were but the vanguards of the great movement to come later. Their operations were certainly neither large nor important at first, but they were undoubtedly pathbreakers who pointed the way to those who were to follow. Tempted by the high prices of cattle and beef in the years following the close of the Civil War, individuals and cattle companies began to penetrate the plains region and establish ranches stocked with young steers from Texas which were often purchased at the cow towns of Kansas.

While the homestead law was in the end to prove the greatest factor in the collapse of the range industry, it was at first of real benefit to the ranchmen. Those wishing to establish ranches would choose a suitable location for a headquarters on one of the numerous streams which traversed the prairies and enter a hundred and sixty acre homestead at some strategic point on it upon which the ranch house and corrals were erected. The various cow hands were then induced to choose homesteads up and down the stream thus securing control of the water supply. Once this was done the back country for many miles on either side could be grazed without fear of interference by others. About the border of the range, line camps were established at convenient intervals where cow hands were stationed to ride the line, look after the cattle, and so far as possible keep them within the limits of their own boundaries.

Many individuals entered the range cattle business, but it soon became apparent that large-scale operations were just as profitable as modest ranching enterprises, and, in many cases, more so. Thus, numerous cattle companies were formed that through organization and clever business management were able to reduce expenses and increase profits. Like the earlier fur traders who sought to avoid competition by reaching out to remote and hitherto unworked areas, so did the ranchmen begin to extend their operations farther and farther west to virgin pasture lands. Here the grass grew thick and rank and here they could have first choice of range and pasture their herds undisturbed by the presence of neighbors.

Yet the firstcomers were quickly followed by others, the boundaries of each man's pasture land being determined by that unwritten law of the range known as "cow custom."

This decreed that the first occupation of a range entitled the occupant to a right to its use. Ranges were therefore held in much the same fashion that lands had been held farther east in an earlier day—by what was known as "squatters rights" or "tomahawk rights." There was, however, a notable difference in that the cattlemen laid no claim to the soil itself, except in the case of the small areas homesteaded, but only to the grass and water.

This was the situation on the public domain, but on Indian reservations there were additional complications. Trespass upon Indian lands was forbidden by law, but where ranges were held on the public domain adjoining them the cattle naturally strayed across the imaginary boundary line of the reservation. Cattlemen, moreover, often made arrangements with the Indian agent and the tribesmen themselves to pasture herds on the reservation and even to establish line camps there offering compensation to the ever hungry Indians in the form of beef or money. No doubt, too, venal agents often received generous sums for ignoring the presence of cattle on reservations under their jurisdiction or for influencing their charges to permit herds to be pastured there. Enterprising ranchmen often eagerly courted the favor of Indians occupying large areas of good pasture lands, their efforts in that direction being not unlike those of European nations who formerly sought spheres of influence among the savage tribes of Africa.

By 1880 the enthusiasm for ranching which has previously been described as "amounting almost to a craze" had swept over the entire country and had even extended itself to Great Britain and the continent of Europe. No scientific attempt has ever been made to determine the original homeland of the western ranchmen and their riders, but it seems likely that they came from virtually every part of this country. Large companies were formed not only to engage in ranching but to finance the operations of others. United States senators, members of Congress, Supreme Court judges, and prominent bankers, lawyers, or physicians were either directly or indirectly interested in the range cattle industry. Credit channels were established between the Great Plains and the financial centers of the East, and many large eastern banks made huge loans to cattle companies or individual ranchmen, while "stockyard banks" were founded at marketing centers and often specialized in "cattle paper." Representatives of some of the oldest and most aristocratic families of the East invested money in ranching enterprises and in some cases came West to give their personal attention to the business.

In time there developed on the western plains a curious American feudalism strongly reminiscent of the feudal order of medieval Europe. The headquarters ranch house of the great ranchman might be neither large nor pretentious and yet as the central point for the administration of a wide region it was not entirely unlike the castle of some medieval landgrave. His cattle ranged over an extent of territory larger than that held by many a German princeling. His riders were quite as numerous as the knights and men at arms of the feudal baron. His brand or distinguishing mark—the *spur, pitchfork, rocking chair, flying H, three circles,* or the *jingle bob*—might be even more widely known than was the bleeding heart of the Douglases, the white lion of the Howards, the clenched hand and dagger of the Kilpatricks, or the blue falcon of Marmion.

Conflicts between rival groups of ranchmen as in Johnson County and Lincoln County wars were not entirely unlike the border wars of Scotland, and the hardy "gunmen" imported for the specific purpose of clearing out "rustlers" or cattle thieves bore some resemblance to the bold "moss troopers" that rode the wide moors and heather-clad hills of north Britain. Meetings with certain similarities to the "folk moot" were called at times to decide important questions, and cases were tried before boards of arbitration in much the same fashion as in the "leet courts" of the Middle Ages. Chivalry, in the original and truest sense of the term, prevailed; for though the range rider was not sworn to protect pure womanhood, he would probably go farther in that direction than did the cavaliers of that older age "when knighthood was in flower." Tests of skill and prowess were also in order, for though the pastoral empire had no tilts or tournaments, the rodeo or roping contest furnished a very satisfactory substitute. Certain bad men appeared in the Cow Country and in time the half legendary figures of Billy the Kid, Clay Allison, John Wesley Hardin, Tom Starr, Sam Bass, Bill Doolin, and the Daltons became clothed with the same glamour of romance which clusters about the names of Robin Hood, Rob Roy, and Rinaldo Rinaldini. Some parallel may even be found between such organizations as the great livestock associations and the Templars, Hospitalers, and Knights of Jerusalem. Both types of organization had great power and influence, extended over a wide region, and at times seemed almost to overshadow the regularly constituted authority of government.

The formation of these great livestock associations was a natural outgrowth of the spread of the empire of grass. Like most institutions they grew out of necessity. Their forebears were the Mayflower Compact, the Land Claims Associations of the middle western states, and the mining camp combinations of California or the Rocky Mountains. In some respects they may be likened to the Sons of Liberty, or the more modern farmer and labor organizations. They were designed, however, not to promote personal liberties but to protect property in a region remote from the ordinary protection of law and courts, property which was by its nature peculiarly vulnerable to depredation and attack. They were, then, economic rather than political in their nature and foreshadowed the future associational arrangements of "Big Business" which sought to act as corporate persons in accordance with frontier ideals. But, though formed on an economic basis, the great livestock associations inevitably soon found themselves engaged in political activity in order to secure legislation favorable to the cattle industry or to prevent the enactment of laws prejudicial to their interests.

Cow custom went far beyond merely defining the limits of each man's or cattle company's range. It must deal with such matters as water rights, the disposal of "mavericks," or unbranded cattle, fencing, quarantine regulations, the inspection of trail herds, the time and manner of conducting roundups, and a score of other matters. Obviously, cow custom must so far as possible be translated into actual law by the state, territory, and nation, and the livestock associations became in time a powerful factor in bringing this about.

At all times the cattle barons must solve grave problems, face many dangers, and combat numerous hostile elements. Thieves and predatory animals were ever ready to take toll of their herds; prairie fires, unless speedily checked, might prove disastrous by destroying wide areas of winter range; the encroachments of sheepmen or settlers must be resisted; and hostile legislation must be checked if possible. Definite rules must be made for roundups, and the boundaries of roundup districts defined. Regulations must be made for the inspection of trail herds, and the registering of brands; breeding must be promoted, and credit channels established. It was to aid in achieving all of these objectives and a hundred more that the livestock associations were established.

One of the greatest of these was the Wyoming Stock Growers Association formed in 1873 with a membership of ten men owning about twenty thousand head of cattle. Within twelve years it had not only spread over the entire state, but had also extended into Colorado, Montana, Nebraska, and Dakota and had a total membership of more than four hundred owning some two million head. Largely through its influence laws were enacted by the Territory of Wyoming relative to branding and driving cattle and even to the time and manner of holding roundups. In time this association became almost an instrumentality of the Territorial government. The time of its annual meeting was fixed by statute, and laws were enacted defining mavericks and providing for their disposition, and covering nearly every other activity of the range cattle industry.

Another very great organization was the Texas and Southwestern Cattle Raisers Association. Established in northern Texas in 1877, it eventually extended to the Indian Territory and New Mexico and even had members in Kansas, Colorado, and some other states. It did much to promote the interests of its far-flung membership and finally became one of the greatest organizations of its kind in the world.

A third cattleman's association and one well worthy of serious consideration was the Cherokee Strip Live Stock Association incorporated under the laws of Kansas in 1883. It was of such a peculiar nature, however, as to seem to deserve special detailed treatment, so an entire subsequent chapter is given to its organization and activities.

The associations named are typical of a great many others of similar nature. They were among the most important though others existed almost, if not quite, as large and a great many smaller ones, some being only of local significance. In all cases the purposes were essentially the same and their methods of operation seldom varied to any considerable degree.

Such organizations were of enormous benefit to the range cattle industry; in fact, it is difficult to see how the great empire of grass could have existed and carried on its activities without them. They made broad rules and regulations to safeguard the interests of their members and to give their property adequate protection. They paid rewards for the scalps of wolves and other predatory animals, and for the arrest and conviction of cattle and horse thieves. They maintained inspectors at the trail crossings of the rivers to examine herds driven north and cut out from them any animals belonging to association members. Other inspectors were stationed at the market centers to check rail shipments of cattle for animals belonging to association members or to assist such members in marketing their own shipments. Still other inspectors rode the ranges, heavily armed to watch for thieves, or to gather evidence of cattle stealing and assist the local peace officers in the apprehension of such criminals. These inspectors eventually developed a code of their own not unlike that of the Northwest Mounted Police or the Texas Rangers. If one were killed in the line of duty his comrades were bound by tradition never to relax their efforts until they "got the man" responsible for his death. The association also employed a legal staff of one or more attorneys charged with the responsibility of prosecuting persons accused of crimes against property under its protection, and of giving legal advice and help to members with respect to civil controversies. In many cases it also published a monthly magazine or association organ, in which was given information on questions affecting the livestock industry. This included such things as records of sales with prices, items concerning market and range conditions, helpful hints on breeding, feeding, and ranch management, general news of the range area, and often historical sketches or reminiscences of oldtime ranchmen.

As already indicated, such organizations were absolutely necessary in carrying on the range cattle industry. Yet, they were perhaps a factor in the formation of a class consciousness which was later to become apparent in the struggle between cattlemen and sheepmen as well as between the ranchmen and the settlers. Also, when such matters as the disposal or fencing of the public domain and leasing or opening to settlement of Indian reservations became the subject of Congressional or departmental action, they were, as already indicated, inevitably forced into political controversies. This led to the accusation that they had been formed largely for political purposes and made them for a time the objects of suspicion and hostility on the part of governmental officials and even a considerable share of the public at large.

Such accusations were largely speaking untrue. Congress, composed largely of members from eastern states, had no adequate conception of the ranchman's problems and frequently proposed legislation that was ill-considered and often little short of absurd. The same lack of understanding was also often shown by officials of the executive departments of the national government. Legislatures and administrative officers of the range states and Territories, of course, knew far more of actual conditions in the pastoral area than did Congress or United States officials, but as settlers poured westward to the plains they soon came to outnumber the range riders. In consequence state and Territorial legislators and other officers yielded, in many cases, to political expediency and with an eager eye to votes were likely to take the side of the settler against that of the ranchman when the interests or even the prejudices of the two seemed to clash. Burdensome quarantine and inspection regulations were enacted or proposed and the question of "herd law" sometimes became a vital issue. Obviously the livestock associations could not be expected to sit idly by while laws were made or regulations imposed that threatened to hamper or even destroy the range industry. The fact remains, however, that they were formed primarily for economic reasons and the political activities which they carried on were incidental to this original purpose.

One factor which greatly increased the prosperity of the cattleman's empire was the improvement of the quality of its cattle. The great livestock associations were, of course, deeply interested in this, but the greater part of the credit for higher grade animals on the plains must be given to individual breeders. Most of the cattle driven north out of Texas for the first few years were the lean, long-horned animals whose forebears were the Spanish cattle brought over by Cortez and other early Spaniards. Though extremely hardy, they were wild and hard to manage and when slaughtered yielded a comparatively low percentage of merchantable beef and that, moreover, was of inferior quality. If the animals were driven north when young

and matured for two or three years on the northern ranges
they grew fatter and heavier than those retained in the South
but even so quantity and quality of beef per head still left
much to be desired. Enterprising ranchmen were quick to
see the advantage of better bred cattle and such men as
Alex Swan, Conrad Kohrs, John Clay, Murdo MacKenzie,
Dan Waggoner, and, in fact, nearly every great ranchman,
began to purchase registered or high-grade breeding animals
in order to improve their herds. Texas, with Indian Territory, Kansas, and parts of New Mexico, remained the better
breeding grounds owing to their warmer climate and lower
altitudes, but breeding herds were also established on ranges
farther north. Experiments made with various breeds at
last resulted in an overwhelming majority of ranchmen
favoring the Hereford as the breed best adapted to plains
conditions, though a few stubbornly urged the superiority
of the Shorthorn or some other type.

   W. S. Ikard is credited with having brought the first Herefords to Texas, but the results were for a time disappoint-
ing. Most of the animals first brought in died of Texas fever,
though they were soon replaced by others, and eventually
registered, or high grade, bulls purchased in the stock farming states of Iowa, Illinois, and Missouri, or even from farther east, were brought to virtually every part of the Cow
Country. White-faced calves began to dot the range and
within a few years the former longhorns had been largely
replaced by a far heavier and better type of cattle. In 1882
it was stated that one ranching firm in Wyoming had purchased $20,000 worth of purebred bulls from a single breeder
in Illinois and that hundreds of ranchmen in Texas had only
purebred bulls with their herds. In the decade from 1873
to 1883 the average weight of cattle slaughtered for beef in

Wyoming had risen from 700 to 880 pounds, in Dakota from 650 to 875 pounds, and in Colorado from 675 to 825 pounds. This increase in weight was due largely to improvement of blood and is even more remarkable when it is considered that most cattle were slaughtered at an earlier age in 1883 than had been the case ten years earlier.

Improvement in breeds was greatly fostered by the growing demand for a better quality of beef. In the years immediately following the war, beef was scarce and the public by no means overparticular. Also, the United States Indian Bureau was a great purchaser of beef as the buffalo disappeared from the ranges and the Indians must be fed. It is true, as has been said, that sales to the Indian Bureau did not account for any great percentage of the cattle marketed for slaughter from the plains area and yet fifty million pounds annually, which was about the quantity eventually purchased for consumption by the reservation Indians, is an imposing figure. Naturally, to the Indian quality was of no great importance. As an export trade developed, however, and new industries swelled the population of many cities, a more discriminating class of customers began to demand better beef than that furnished by the lean, rawboned Texas longhorns. Also, as cattle spread over the plains and range grew scarce it became imperative that cattle be marketed at an earlier age than formerly since Texas steers were sometimes not sent to slaughter until they were six or seven years old. Better breeds meant earlier marketing and range conservation, as well as a better quality of beef and higher prices.

Better breeding was promoted also by the invention and widespread use of barbed wire. A patent for one type had been issued as early as 1868 but not until 1875 did two salesmen for the first manufacturer, Joseph Glidden, appear in

Texas. At first they met with scant success but eventually established an agency at Houston for marketing their product throughout the state. Within a few years the ranchmen began to see the advantages of fencing and this agency was selling barbed wire to the amount of $750,000 annually.

Barbed wire almost revolutionized the cattle industry in Texas, where liberal land laws made it possible to secure title to large tracts of land in fee and to lease others for a long term of years. It reduced the number of workers necessary to care for cattle, promoted the conservation of range, and encouraged the purchase of breeding animals, since with fenced pastures the owner could be insured the exclusive use of them. Yet, it created new problems as well. "Fence cutting wars" broke out, and bill after bill was introduced in the Texas legislature forbidding the use of barbed wire for fencing though none of these was ever enacted into law.

The use of the new fencing material also spread rapidly to the central and northern plains and there, too, it created new problems. The erection of wire fences on the public domain was prohibited by act of Congress and was for a time either forbidden or greatly restricted on Indian reservations by orders of the Department of the Interior. Yet both the statute and the departmental orders were often violated by ranchmen. Lands owned in fee or leased from the railways could, moreover, be fenced without complications and on these breeding ranches were established to provide high-grade bulls for the open ranges.

As the enthusiasm for ranching grew and the apparently never-ending stream of Texas cattle continued to pour north and spread over the plains, pasture lands began to grow scarce. In fact, by the middle eighties most of the range was fully stocked and much of it overstocked. For such over-stocking a part of the blame must be laid at the doors of Congress, which failed to make any provision for long-term grazing leases on that part of the public domain which would clearly not be required for settlement by home-steaders for many years in the future. Fearful of the pre-carious and uncertain tenure of their ranges, many men exploited them by bringing in more cattle than they could support in adequate fashion for any considerable time. As a result the grass was cropped close and the foundations laid for the first great tragedy—the terrible winter of 1886-87 —and for the later tragic problems incident to soil erosion by wind and water.

With range growing scarce, efforts were made to open up new lands to grazing. Large areas of the Great Plains could not originally be pastured because of lack of water. In 1880 it was stated that nearly half of the Staked Plains of Texas was unwatered and that no less than twenty-nine million acres of land in that state were entirely unavailable for grazing because of the lack of an adequate water supply. Doubtless the same situation prevailed in a somewhat less degree to the central and northern plains. Cattle will not ordinarily graze, at most, more than five to ten miles from water, and lands lying farther than that from a permanent water supply are useless for grazing purposes during the greater part of the year.

The invention and widespread use of barbed wire was a powerful factor in adding these lands to the occupied do-main of the cattleman's empire. In most cases water could be supplied by artificial means through the building of dams across ravines to impound the rainfall, and by drilling deep wells and installing windmills. Such methods of providing water are expensive, and men pasturing cattle upon the open range were naturally reluctant to undertake them. Within their own pastures enclosed by wire fences, however, it was a different story. Ranchmen began to purchase or lease these unwatered lands of northwest Texas, fence them, and drill wells which were provided with windmills and steel tanks. One such well would provide water for some three hundred head of cattle. Farther north men pasturing cattle on the public domain would drill wells on lands held as homesteads, or on those leased from railroads. In time most of these hitherto useless lands were made available for grazing and many millions of acres thus added to the domain of the Cow Country.

As has already been indicated, the cattleman's empire of grass had by the middle eighties reached its maximum extent of territory and the height of its importance. It covered by that time a region comparable in size to all of western Europe, upon which grazed more than twelve million head of cattle. Politically, it was an invisible empire in the sense that it wielded great unofficial powers in the legislative halls of both state and national governments. It seemed rich, powerful, and prosperous. Cattle were high, profits great, and it appeared to be entering upon a golden age of still greater prosperity and wealth.

Beneath the surface, however, were elements of weakness which even the most optimistic of the leaders could not fail to observe. It had grown up, mushroom like, upon the prairies without sufficient time to brace and strengthen its structure, stabilize its order, and consolidate its gains. Greed and an eager desire for huge and sudden profits had played far too large a part in its development. As has been noted, most of the range was by this time fully stocked and much of it overstocked. Yet many of the empire's more important figures eagerly sought to expand operations when every sign of the times indicated that they should be retrenched. Much of the business was carried on by means of capital borrowed in the financial centers of the East or from Europe. If the financial assets of the empire had been balanced against its liabilities most of the apparent prosperity would have been revealed as largely a myth.

It had, however, liabilities of other than a financial nature which were equally important. Outside its limits it had but few friends and many enemies and the forces hostile to it were steadily growing stronger. Moreover, it could not present to these a wholly united front. Strong as was the class consciousness of its people, there smoldered between certain elements or regions within its limits fires of jealousy and suspicion that often threatened to burst into flame. With ranges already heavily stocked there was no room for further expansion, and the occupants, often deeply in debt, held the use of their pasture lands by a very shaky and uncertain tenure. Heavy losses of cattle or any sharp decline in prices could hardly fail to prove ruinous. Truly it was an Empire of Grass which had been created in every sense of the term. In fair weather it would stand intact but any heavy, adverse wind was certain to bring it tumbling down about its builders and to the weather wise within its borders it was apparent that the wind was fast rising.

V

Short Grass and Heather

I was born and bred in Scotland
And I love its glens and cairns,
Though I alone have left it
Of all my mother's bairns.
Yes, I left its rugged mountains
And its lakes like shining glass
To seek for fame and fortune
In a land of sky and grass.
Each day I ride the prairies wide
In every kind of weather,
But in my dreams it often seems
I'm back amid the heather.

SCOTTISH RIDERS

ONE OF THE MOST IMPORTANT FACTORS in the growth of the Empire of Grass was the part played in its development by men and money from Great Britain and especially from Scotland. Many millions of dollars in British capital were invested in ranching on the Great Plains, and a considerable number of Scots and Englishmen came over to give their personal attention to the business. For centuries a large part of the "roast beef of merrie England" was raised among the heather clad Scottish hills. During much of the last quarter of the nineteenth century, however, no small part of it originated on the broad plains of the "Short Grass Country." In time the volume of American raised beef poured into the British Isles became so great as to threaten seriously the business of the cattle growers of North Britain, and between them and the ranchmen of our western prairies developed a certain rivalry which might be called a struggle between short grass and heather.

The foreign trade in American beef and cattle, out of which eventually developed British interest in the range cattle industry, originated before the American Revolution. A considerable number of live cattle as well as much salt and pickled beef had been exported from the American

89

colonies, largely to the West Indies, during the eighteenth century. Charleston, South Carolina, exported nearly two thousand barrels of pickled beef in 1747 and five years later Philadelphia was exporting 3,500 barrels annually. Savannah, Georgia, sent a considerable number of live cattle and pickled beef to West Indian ports nearly every year from 1750 to the outbreak of the Revolution.

This trade was checked by the war, but after independence had been won it was quickly resumed and by 1800 the export of salt and pickled beef from the entire country amounted to well over seventy-five thousand barrels annually. The trade then began to decline rapidly owing in part, no doubt, to the Napoleonic wars in Europe and the consequent danger to cargoes on the high seas. After the close of the second war with Great Britain it began to grow again and in time reached considerable proportions.

Soon after its admission to the Union in 1845, Texas began the exportation of cattle and pickled beef to Cuba and other islands of the West Indies. The outbreak of the Civil War put an end to this traffic, but it was resumed in 1865 and an extensive trade soon developed. Indianola and Galveston were the chief exporting points and within a few years shipments averaged from twelve to fifteen hundred head a month. The trip could be made to Cuba in about four days and in consequence losses were in most cases small and profits certain. This trade reached its peak in 1875 when over thirty-three thousand head of cattle with a value of nearly one-half million dollars were exported from Texas. The trade then declined partly because of increased shipments of cattle from Florida to Cuba but largely because the discovery of new methods of refrigeration had made it possible to ship fresh meats from New York to Havana.

Soon after the close of the Civil War an attempt had been made to send live cattle from Texas to England. A company was formed for that purpose and a large shipment was started. The results were disastrous. Hardly 15 per cent of the cargo reached England alive and the animals that had not died on the voyage were so thin and bruised as to be almost worthless. The company abandoned the project in despair and the chief effect of the venture was to prevent any further attempt to ship live cattle to Europe for a number of years.

As the range cattle industry continued to spread over the western plains, however, the high prices for beef and cattle which had prevailed in the years immediately following the Civil War rapidly declined. This, coupled with the knowledge of the high price of beef in England, caused a number of men to begin a series of experiments in refrigeration with the hope of discovering a process which would make it possible to send dressed beef across the Atlantic.

One of these men was John I. Bate, of New York. After several years of diligent experimentation he evolved a process by which the carcasses might be hung in refrigerator rooms and kept at a temperature of about 38° Fahrenheit by means of ice-cooled air circulated among them by huge fans. In February, 1875, Bate prepared to test his plan through a shipment of twelve quarters of beef to England. The steamship company thought so little of his idea, however, that they refused him the use of steam with which to operate the fans. Unwilling to give up the test he hired men to turn them by hand, which must have seemed a most tedious and uninteresting task before the long voyage across the Atlantic had ended. The beef arrived in excellent condition, however, so in June Bate sent over a shipment of ten beeves, having in the meantime prevailed upon the steamship management to provide steam to turn the fans. In August he exported the carcasses of twenty more beeves and 140 sheep. All of his shipments reached England in perfect condition. Bate felt that the success of his method of refrigeration was fully proved and soon after sold out his patent and the right to use the process to Timothy C. Eastman, of New York.

The first shipment made by Eastman was in October, 1875. In that month he shipped thirty-six thousand pounds of dressed beef to England to be followed by an equal quantity in November and 134,000 pounds in December. By April, 1876, his shipments had risen to more than one million pounds a month, by September to more than two million, and by December to more than three million.

It was not long before a number of other individuals and companies began the exportation of refrigerated beef to Great Britain utilizing processes similar to Bate's. Among these were Gillett and Sherman, Samuels and Company, Daniel Toffey and Company, and Snowden and McConville, all shipping from New York and Jersey City, while Martin, Fuller and Company, and Morris and Allerton began shipments from Philadelphia and the Wells Company from Portland, Maine. Shipments were made by the Cunard, Inman, National, Williams and Guion, White Star, and Anchor lines of steamers as well as some others. It was said that for a time nearly every steamer bound from New York or Philadelphia to England carried American beef as a part of its cargo. New experiments were made in refrigeration and the Bate and similar processes revised and improved.

After 1876 exports of dressed beef steadily grew and were supplemented by renewed shipments of live cattle as better

methods were evolved for caring for such animals during
the voyage. In 1877 the quantity of fresh beef exported was
forty-nine million pounds and the number of live cattle
more than fifty thousand head. In 1878 it had grown to more
than fifty million pounds and 136,000 head. In 1884 it was
120,000,000 pounds and 190,000 head of live cattle. Virtually all of these exports were to Great Britain and Ireland,
which normally received about 90 per cent of cattle and
cattle products shipped from the United States, including
canned or salt beef, hides, and tallow.

The chief problem of Eastman and others during the
early years of this trade was not one of transportation but
of obtaining cattle which would furnish beef of the type
demanded by the foreign market. The English consumer
insisted upon fat, heavy beef of high quality and this the
range area could not supply except in limited quantities.
The result was to establish closer relations between the
ranchmen of the Great Plains and the cattle feeders of the
Corn Belt as well as to give a great impetus to breeding
better animals. More and more purebred sires were sent
from the midwestern states to the Cow Country in order
to improve the herds of that region while more and more
young steers of good blood were shipped from the western
ranges to the Corn Belt. Here they were fed on corn for
from six to twelve months and so brought up to the quality
demanded by the export trade. Both of these movements
were encouraged as much as possible by state and federal
agencies for the promotion of agriculture. As early as 1876
the Commissioner of Agriculture published an annual report containing this significant paragraph:

"Let the vast areas of pasture in the border states and
territories be employed for breeding and feeding the cattle

until they are two years old, and then let them be sent forward to the older sections to be fed a year on corn and rounded up to the proportions of the foreign demand."

This coming only a year after the first shipments of dressed beef to Europe is important in showing how quickly had come the realization of the growing importance of foreign trade in beef and cattle.

In the meantime the ever-growing flood of American meat which came pouring into the British Isles created there both joy and consternation. Joy on the part of the consumers who found the price of beef reduced by two or three pence a pound and consternation among the farmers and stock growers, particularly in North Britain, who saw their business threatened and themselves facing ruin.

Markets for American beef were established in London, Liverpool, Manchester, Birmingham, Sheffield, Leeds, New-Castle, Edinburgh, Dundee, Dublin, and other cities. As the supply grew in volume the excitement of the agricultural population of Great Britain increased. Many newspapers carried lengthy articles on the subject of the importation of American meat, and this new trade and the situation it had created became the chief topic of conversation. It was discussed in drawing rooms, about tea tables, and with considerable detail in the halls of Parliament. The Queen, Prince of Wales, Lord Mayor of London, the Governor of the Bank of England, and numerous other persons of importance all endorsed the quality of American meat, and even the butchers who had formerly sold only the home-grown product found no fault with it.

Not a few people, however, influenced perhaps by wishful thinking, asserted that American beef could never hope to compete with that produced in England since it must inevitably be of inferior quality. While the excitement was at its height a number of these critics were invited to dinner at the home of a prominent resident of London. The basis of the dinner was a huge, red roast of beef, which the guests enjoyed to the fullest. As they ate, the conversation turned to the subject of importations of American meat and they were unanimous in the opinion that the British cattle growers had no cause for alarm since it was obvious that America could never produce beef of similar quality. Their chagrin was great when the host told them at the conclusion of the meal that what they had been eating was American-grown beef!

At first some difficulties were experienced in the proper preservation of the cargoes of meat after they reached England. These were overcome by the erection of large refrigerators at ports of entry, each divided into a number of compartments for the storage of carcasses of beef. This eliminated the necessity for immediate distribution and sale regardless of price or the quantity already on hand and so helped to stabilize the market and strengthen the business as a whole.

The concern of the cattle raisers of North Britain became so great that in 1877 the *Scotsman*, a newspaper devoted largely to the agricultural interests of that region, sent to America James MacDonald, a prominent member of its staff, with instructions to visit the range cattle area and other livestock raising portions of the United States and make reports in the form of a series of articles for publication. These articles, which were later republished in a volume entitled *Food from the Far West*, described the ranching industry on the Great Plains and told of the low price of land and of great profits made in cattle raising which, it was asserted, often averaged 25 per cent annually.

These articles served to increase the excitement to such a degree that the British government in the autumn of 1879 sent two commissioners to America to investigate the possibilities of the range cattle industry in an effort to determine whether or not there was likely to be any limit to this great influx of American meat. The men chosen were Clare Read and Albert Pell, both members of Parliament. They were dispatched in response to a Parliamentary resolution passed in 1879 and spent several months in the range states and territories of the West. Their report published in 1880 described in glowing terms the life of the western ranchmen and stated that no capital had been invested in the range cattle industry of America in recent years which had not returned a profit of as much as 33 per cent annually.

The Scottish bankers and moneylenders read this report with an enthusiasm that rapidly mounted to fever heat. They were of a people noted for thrift and business ability and the very thought of 33 per cent annually on an investment was dazzling. The effect in England was hardly less startling, and it was said that the announcement of an important gold discovery could hardly have created greater excitement throughout the Island Kingdom than did this report of Read and Pell. Here was gold to be had almost for the taking by any man courageous enough to invest his money on these western prairies or to go there and engage in a business which was alleged to offer a most pleasant and attractive life as well as such enormous profits.

Canny Scottish and British capitalists had already seen in the range cattle industry of America an attractive field for investment and had formed several companies to finance ranching enterprises in the Great Plains region. In 1872 the

Scottish-American Investment Company had been founded by W. J. Menzies. It financed a number of great cattle companies in the range area including the Wyoming Cattle Ranch Company and Western Ranches Limited. Another very important Scottish syndicate formed quite early in order to finance ranching operations in America was the Scottish-American Mortgage Company. It was under the management of Duncan Smith, a lawyer of Edinburgh. It established the Prairie Cattle Company, one of the largest ranching enterprises in the West. Its three ranges lying in Texas, New Mexico, Colorado, and Kansas embraced a total of some eight thousand square miles of pasture land, part of which was owned in fee, though the greater part was leased. Its cattle numbered at one time 140,000 head and the total value of livestock and improvements on its three ranges was said to be well in excess of four million dollars.

The report of the Parliamentary commissioners not only stimulated enormously the activities of these large investment syndicates already in operation, but brought about the creation of many others large and small. It also directed the attention of many individuals to the opportunities offered by the range cattle industry in America. Some of these decided to come to the United States in order to engage in ranching, while not a few remained at home but financed ranching ventures by others. By 1882 it was estimated that more than thirty million dollars of British capital, most of it from Scotland, had been invested in ranching on the western plains, and during the next three or four years this amount was enormously increased.

In addition to those already mentioned, a large number of important cattle companies were founded by Scottish capital. These included the Matador, Hansford Land and

Cattle Company, Texas Land and Cattle Company, Powder River Cattle Company, and many others. Not a few of the investors came to America to give their personal attention to the business, while others merely sent over trusted agents.

It is doubtful that any other individual had as much to do with foreign investments in ranching as did John Clay, Jr. Born in Scotland in 1851, he came to America for the first time in 1874 and returned in 1879 with the Read and Pell commission, which he served in the capacity of secretary, or subcommissioner. For the next three years he remained in the employment of the British government making studies of livestock conditions in the United States and Canada. His family owned a small share in the Bow Park Stock Farm in Ontario, which specialized in the raising of pedigreed livestock and imported fine breeding animals from Great Britain. Clay eventually became manager of this farm and attended many fairs and livestock shows in the United States and Canada for the purpose of exhibiting Bow Park animals. Here he met many western ranchmen and sought to interest them in better bred livestock and himself became interested in ranching on the western plains.

Clay soon became the agent of several investment companies both Scottish and English and gave up his work at Bow Park to travel extensively throughout the range area examining ranch properties and reporting upon prospective loans and purchases or on those that had already been made. As agent for the Scottish-American Investment Company, he was largely instrumental in the founding by means of British capital such enterprises as the Wyoming Cattle Ranch Company, the Cattle Ranch and Land Company, Western Ranches Limited, and various others.

He also assisted in the organization of the Swan Land and

Cattle Company, one of the largest of the ranching ventures on the plains financed by Scottish capital. It combined three large properties originally belonging to an American concern known as Swan and Frank, in which Alex H. Swan and Joseph Frank were the chief figures. The company was formed with a capital stock of three million dollars. The number of cattle according to book count numbered eighty-nine thousand head pastured largely on the public domain though a considerable area of deeded land had been secured and to this the company soon added more than one-half million acres additional in alternate sections purchased from the Union Pacific Railroad. The capital stock was also later increased by three quarters of a million dollars, most of which was expended in the purchase of land. Alex Swan failed in 1887 and the Scottish investors were compelled to take over and administer the property. Eventually Clay was made manager and served in that position for some eight years, succeeding at last in putting the enterprise upon a paying basis once more. Still later Clay founded the John Clay Live Stock Commission Company with offices at all of the principal market centers of the country, which became one of the greatest organizations of its kind in America.

Another of the great figures among the Scots engaged in the range cattle industry of America was Murdo MacKenzie, whose name must forever be linked with that of the great Scottish cattle company known as the Matador. He was born in County Ross, Scotland, in 1850. He came to the United States in 1885 and served as manager of the Prairie Cattle Company from that date until 1890. The following year he became manager of the Matador Land and Cattle Company in northwest Texas, which had been founded as a Scottish concern in 1882 with a capital stock of two and one-half million dollars. The original Matador Ranch, however, had been established four years earlier by an American, H. H. Campbell, who was retained by the Scottish company as manager until 1891.

The Matador herds were originally pastured largely upon the public domain of the state of Texas but by 1891, when MacKenzie became manager, the company owned in fee about 540,000 acres of land and had some two hundred thousand acres more under lease. Later a breeding ranch was established in Oldham County, Texas, by the purchase of 227,000 acres of land to which an additional 120,000 acres were eventually added. The Matador at one time had more than one hundred thousand head of cattle, but the growing scarcity of range caused them in later years to reduce this number to about seventy thousand head. Large areas of pasture land were leased in Montana as a finishing range to which young steers bred in Texas were sent to be matured. MacKenzie remained general manager of the Matador for nearly forty years except for a brief period when he left it to assume charge of some ranch properties in South America. Largely because of his interest in better-bred animals, he built up the quality of the animals on the ranch until Matador Herefords came to rank among the finest cattle in the world.

While the men and companies of Scottish origin that have been named were among the most important of those operating upon the Great Plains, there were many others. Not a few individual Scots were engaged in ranching enterprises or were in the employ of others. Also large numbers of English and a considerable number of Irish came to the plains to establish themselves in the range cattle business, and huge sums of English capital were invested in the industry. In fact it is not always possible to separate entirely the English and Scottish companies since nearly every company might have both English and Scottish shareholders.

Between the Scots and the English who actually came to the plains to engage in ranching, however, there was, broadly speaking, one notable difference. Virtually all of the former were clever, hardheaded businessmen engaged in the range cattle industry for the profits which might be derived from it, while not a few of the latter were members of the nobility or their younger sons who found in it an agreeable, adventurous life and seemed not to care so much for financial returns. This idea must not be developed too far since there were many Englishmen and English concerns that were quite as aggressive and businesslike as were those of Scottish origin, but the "gentleman rancher" apparently in search of adventure was common among the English whereas he scarcely appears at all among the Scots.

Some of the titled Englishmen who had large landholdings in the West upon which they grazed cattle were Lord Dunraven, who owned the larger part of the present Estes Park, Colorado; the Marquis of Tweesdale, who is said to have held title to 1,750,000 acres; Lord Dunmore, with 100,000 acres; and a number of others. Some of these men sought to bring something of an Old World type of life to these western prairies. They built expensive ranch houses, fitted with furnishings from Britain, imported English servants, and laid in large stocks of liquors. They entertained large parties of guests who came out each summer on hunting and fishing trips, and many of them continued to read regularly the London papers and to look upon England as home. Of course these were more or less exceptional, but large numbers of individual Englishmen were engaged in ranching on the plains and a rather large part of these always retained, to a greater or less degree, their Old World characteristics.

A considerable number of great cattle companies were also financed wholly or in part by English or Irish capital. Among these were the Espuela, or Spur, Ranch, founded by Americans, sold to an English syndicate, and later resold to S. M. Swenson, becoming the S. M. S. Ranch of today. The Carlisle Cattle Company in Wyoming was also an English concern, as was the L X Ranch of northwest Texas. Other important concerns financed wholly or in part by English money were the Rocking Chair Ranch and the American Pastoral Company. Also, the great X I T, or Capitol Syndicate Ranch, of three and one-half million acres and 160,000 head of cattle, was largely developed and improved by funds secured from an English company organized for that specific purpose. This was the Capitol Freehold and Investment Company formed in London in 1885. It sold bonds to raise the necessary money, the first sale amounting to one million pounds sterling. The English directors, however, had no part in directing the affairs of the ranch itself, and the bondholders were not shareholders in the ranch but merely in the company, receiving their interest on the bonds regardless of whether or not the X I T paid dividends. Not until 1909 were the bonds retired and the English company dissolved. It had made possible the creation of this vast ranching enterprise on the land given by the state of Texas in payment for the erection of its magnificent state capitol. Still another important ranch founded in northwest Texas by British capital was the J. A., established by General John G. Adair in 1876. General Adair was of Scotch-Irish descent, however, and had large landholdings in Ireland so this ranch might properly be said to have been founded with Irish, rather than English, capital.

The excitement over ranching ventures on the western plains which swept over the British Isles following the great importation of American meat and the report of Read and Pell soon extended to the Continent with the result that a number of well-known Continental figures soon appeared among the ranchmen of the range cattle area. Prominent among these was Walter, Baron von Richthofen, ancestor of the noted "Red Knight of Germany," so famous during the First World War. He established himself on a range in Colorado and later wrote a small book called *Cattle Ranching on the Plains of North America.*

The most picturesque of all the Continentals to engage in cattle raising in America, however, was the French nobleman, Antoine de Vallambrosa, Marquis de Mores. He came to New York in 1882, where he married Medora von Hoffman, daughter of a wealthy banker of German descent. Of an adventurous nature, de Mores became deeply interested in cattle raising in the West and in 1883 went to Dakota Territory, where he set up a ranch on the Little Missouri River, presumably largely with his father-in-law's money. Here he engaged in a rivalry with young Theodore Roosevelt, who had established the Elkhorn Ranch in the same region, each of them seeking to make himself the dominant figure among the cattlemen of this portion of Dakota. It is doubtful that either of them knew, or ever learned, too much of a practical nature about ranching, but de Mores was a visionary of the most extreme type. On a hill overlooking the bleak wastes of the "Bad Lands" he erected a magnificent chateau in which he and his wife lived for the next three or four years. He established a packing plant and hoped to control the beef trade of the entire Northwest.

The scheme was utterly foolish since he could not hope to secure any but grass-fed cattle and these only for three or four months in the year. He founded the town of Medora, named for his wife, and established the Medora to Deadwood Stage Line, which also proved impracticable and was soon abandoned. He fenced his ranch at great expense when everyone else was pasturing cattle on the open range and neglected his cattle in order to engage in big game hunting. He had a number of ambitious schemes for making vast profits, all of which proved failures. It has been said that he squandered a total of $1,500,000 in his ill-starred ranching venture.

Another French ranchman, but of a far different type, was Pierre Wibaux, for whom the town of Wibaux, Montana, was named. He came to America in 1883 and established a ranch partly in Montana and partly in Dakota. Starting in a small way he in time came to own sixty-five thousand head of cattle. His great ranch house built in 1890 and called the "White House," or "Palace," was one of the show places of the Northwest, at which he and his wife entertained hundreds of guests from every part of the country and not a few from Europe. Wibaux sold the ranch and retired from the cattle business in 1904.

It must be clear to any student of the range cattle industry that men and money from Europe played an enormous part in its development. It must be equally apparent that European interest in it was largely an outgrowth of our shipments of dressed beef to the British Isles and that of the Old World elements which entered the business the Scots were by far the most important. Not only were Scots the pioneers among the Europeans engaged in ranching and the promotion of ranching enterprises in America but from Scotland came a very large share of the foreign capital invested in cattle raising on the Great Plains. The Scots also did more than any other group toward improving the quality of the animals pastured in the range area. Accustomed to fine cattle in their own country, and highly skilled in scientific breeding, they could not endure the thought of devoting their energies to raising the wild, long-horned Texas cattle which originally covered the plains in such vast numbers. It was largely through the efforts of the Scots that the Great Plains area eventually came to have cattle immeasurably superior to those of most other parts of the United States. Most important of all, perhaps, they brought to the cattlemen's empire of grass rare business ability, thrift, foresight, and sound judgment, qualities which the ranching industry sorely needed and had hitherto largely lacked.

Important as was their personal and financial help in the development of the range cattle industry, however, the coming of the Scots and other Europeans to the plains area was not altogether an unmixed blessing. There can be little doubt that their presence helped to swell the growing hostility to the livestock interests of the West. As the homesteaders began to penetrate the plains in ever-increasing numbers, bitter criticisms were voiced in Congress and elsewhere of these "rich and insolent foreigners who monopolize the public domain and seek to discourage its settlement by poor but honest farmers in search of homes." Largely speaking, such criticism was seldom deserved, but it grew in volume and eventually brought the entire industry into bad repute with a considerable portion of the American public, from which it never entirely recovered.

It will be observed that but few Europeans and comparatively little foreign capital entered the range cattle business until about the close of the seventies or the very early eighties, a time when the enthusiasm for ranching sweeping over the country had extended beyond our shores to become almost world-wide in scope. The industry was at that time growing rapidly and seemed very prosperous. Most of the Scots and other foreigners entered it barely in time to share for a very brief period in this prosperity. All too soon they were to share in its adversity as well and for its downfall must bear a certain measure of responsibility.

As has been previously indicated the industry reached the height of its prosperity and importance about 1885. At that time cattle were high, and everyone, on paper at least, seemed to be making large profits. But the unseen specter of disaster was riding boot to boot with many a ranchman of the western prairies. Easy money and the hope of sudden riches had led most men into reckless borrowing and great over-stocking of their ranges. They had sown the wind and were very soon to reap the whirlwind. Clouds which should have given warning of the coming storm were in 1885 already beginning to cast their ominous shadows over the plains, but in most cases were unheeded. Yet the tempest was soon to break and even the rare ability of the canny Scots could not delay its coming or check its fury.

The winter of 1885 was on the whole not particularly severe, but heavy rains fell throughout most of the Great Plains area during the late autumn, which, in the language of the range, "soaked the strength out of the grass" thereby greatly reducing its value as winter pasturage. To this was attributed the fact that there were considerable losses dur-ing this winter and that most cattle were in poor condition in the spring. Perhaps the reason given was largely a myth. It seems more likely that the range was overstocked to a far greater degree than was realized and that this was the chief cause of loss and of thin cattle in the spring. Also, more than two hundred thousand head of cattle had been removed from the Cheyenne-Arapaho Indian reservation at the beginning of winter by order of President Cleveland. These had to be placed upon ranges in adjoining states that were already heavily grazed, with the result that all cattle in that region in particular had insufficient pasturage.

These things were all forgotten with the coming of warm weather, and the ranchmen's hopes rose with the springing grass that began to clothe the prairies with a coat of green. Cattle were still high, the calf crop on the southern plains was good, and the future seemed rosy. As soon as spring was sufficiently advanced that cattle might be set in motion, tens of thousands of head were driven north and spread over the heavily stocked ranges of the northern plains in the most reckless fashion imaginable, the owners staking the lives of the animals on the uncertain hazard that the coming winter would be a mild one.

Then came the never to be forgotten "tragedy of eighty-six and seven"! Very early winter swept down out of the frozen North and laid its icy hand upon the northern prairies. A terrific snowstorm swept over the plains and the thermometer went down as though it would never stop. Snow succeeded snow and blizzard followed blizzard. The cattle drifted before the bitter wind into the canyons and coulees where they died by thousands and tens of thousands. Years later riders pointed out the dry willows along the streams killed by the hunger-maddened animals that had gnawed the bark from them as high as they could reach before they at last gave up the struggle and lay down to die. Ranchmen gathered about the great fireplaces of the cattlemen's club in Cheyenne sought to console one another by the remark: "Never mind boys, after all the books won't freeze." They soon discovered that book count in selling cattle was a thing of the past. Spring came to find virtually every large operator on the northern plains flat broke. Conrad Kohrs, Alex Swan, Dickey Brothers—all of the great ranchmen, in fact—were either bankrupt or in dire distress. Smaller ones who in many cases had "started on a shoestring" saw all of their original capital and most of their borrowed capital scattered about over the frozen prairie, food for the wolves. In a very real sense their assets were frozen with no hope that they could ever be thawed.

Charles Russell, the cowboy artist, was in charge of a herd of five thousand head that had been purchased by some eastern investors. As winter drew to a close his employers wrote him a letter asking how the cattle were doing. Russell painted a picture which has since become famous and sent it as his reply. It depicted one lonely old steer standing in deep showdrifts like some bovine Peri at the very gates of Paradise and beneath it the artist had written the title *The Last of Five Thousand*.

The range cattle industry never recovered from that terrible winter of 1886–87, with which no other in the memory of the oldest inhabitants could even remotely compare. Most of the foreigners, stunned by their losses, gave it up in despair as did virtually all of the Americans who had entered the business more or less as an adventure. The Marquis de Mores abandoned all of his fantastic schemes and sailed for France eventually to lose his life on an ill-starred expedition to the interior of Africa. Young Theodore Roosevelt returned to New York to engage in politics, leaving the ranges of the Elkhorn thickly strewn with bones.

To make matters worse, the summer of 1887 was extremely dry in the corn-producing states and the crop was almost a total failure. As a result there was no demand for feeder cattle, and the foreign market had also greatly decreased. Yet holders of "cattle paper" were clamorous in their demands for the repayment of their loans and to raise money numerous ranchmen began to pour thin, underweight cattle into Chicago, Kansas City, and other market centers. The market sagged and finally completely collapsed. Cattle that would have brought high prices a year earlier by the autumn of 1887 would hardly be accepted as a gift.

Though heavy losses extended as far south as Kansas and Indian Territory, Texas, naturally, largely escaped them. Yet the southern ranchmen could not escape the effect of low prices, the disappearance of any northern market, and the general depression of the industry as a whole. Investors had become so frightened that they refused to make further loans on cattle even in the South and demanded the repayment of those in force as fast as they fell due. True, the southern ranchmen still had their cattle but markets had vanished, their herds were increasing, and the range, already overstocked, was rapidly reduced during the next few years by the westward advance of homesteaders and the opening to settlement of most of the great Indian reservations in western Oklahoma. As a result they too were in distress.

Those who know intimately the story can hardly fail to marvel at the courage with which many of the ranchmen of the Great Plains faced the future. While most of the Scots in common with other Europeans gave up the struggle, there were some notable exceptions. The Swan Cattle Company, under the management of John Clay, and the Matador, under that of Murdo MacKenzie, still carried on and remain today as monuments to the business genius of these two great men and the faith and daring of the Scottish investors. The former company, however, eventually gave up cattle raising for the less speculative and picturesque, but more profitable, business of raising sheep, leaving the Matador as the only great cattle ranching enterprise of Scottish origin now in the United States. Not a few of the Scots still remain in America as herd masters of operators specializing in registered cattle, but many of them returned home, where they and the investors who had financed their operations in the Short Grass Country have contented themselves with small but certain profits to be found in raising cattle on the heather-clad hills of their native land.

The fearful winter of 1886–87 by no means put an end to the range cattle industry on the western plains. In fact it still flourishes in some areas of the West, but that date marked the end of an era and the dawn of a new day. From that time it was apparent that year-round grazing on the northern plains was a myth. It was plain, too, that in the future retrenchment, rather than expansion, must be the rule. Smaller-scale operations and fenced pastures began to take the place of the former huge enterprises which had largely used the public domain for pasture land. It was clear also that better-bred animals, which could be marketed for slaughter at an earlier age, must be grown in order to conserve range. For the range was fast shrinking. A flood of settlers was pouring westward to take up homesteads, and this was not to end until every part of the public domain suitable for cultivation had been occupied and the remaining ranchmen forced to abandon all lands not owned in fee and retire to the barren hills or the arid region farther west, where crops could not be grown except by irrigation.

Part IV

The Human Pattern

VI

Riders of the Range

My home is my saddle
My roof is the sky;
The prairies I'll ride
Till the day that I die.
I'll live on the prairie
Till life shall have passed
And lie down to sleep
In her bosom at last.

SADDLE SONG

SOMEONE HAS SAID THAT THE WEST has been the mother of many children. Prominent among her offspring were the trapper, fur trader, prospector, freighter, cowboy, and homesteader. One by one these sons of a great mother were born, each lived out his allotted life span and passed away, and with the passing of the last one the mother herself must die. Each of these has had his biographers, but far more than his brothers has the range rider of the Cow Country caught the fancy and attracted the interest of a later generation. Of him and his vocation much has been written, and yet few people who know at first hand something of ranching on the western plains are willing to admit that any book on the subject is entirely correct. This is due largely to the fact that the range cattle industry came into being suddenly, rose to mammoth proportions, and, except in certain isolated areas, largely disappeared within a single generation. In consequence, it never became fully standardized and conditions varied widely in the different portions of that widespread region commonly called the Cow Country. Certainly the life and problems of the rider of the "brush country" of Texas or the cactus-covered semideserts of Arizona were considerably unlike those of his contemporary on the northern plains of Montana or the Dakotas, and yet there were many factors common to both.

With the exception of the fur trade no other industry of the Great West required so few men for its successful operation throughout a wide area as did ranching on the open range, and no other employed so few men in proportion to the amount of capital invested. The lean, muscular riders of the range were never at any one time very numerous, though the great pastoral empire in which they carried on their work was larger than all of western Europe.

The leading ranchmen are often described as men who knew the cattle business in all of its details with the inference that they seldom knew much of anything else. "Old man John Chisum knew cows" was an oft repeated phrase in the Southwest. As a matter of fact many, if not most, of the great ranchers were men of education, real business judgment, and executive ability. They sometimes owned herds of cattle valued at more than a million dollars and controlled lands of enormous extent. They bought and sold many thousand head of animals each year and had many employees on their pay rolls. They improved breeds, sought to influence legislation in the state or nation, practiced the arts of diplomacy in dealing with Indian tribes or government officials, opened up credit channels to financial centers of the East, and were among the first captains of industry of the Great Plains.

Comparatively little has been written about the great leaders of the range cattle industry in America, but they played a most important part in the history of the West. When the full story is written the names of such men as Richard King, John Iliff, Charles Goodnight, Ike Pryor, Murdo MacKenzie, John Clay, Dan Waggoner, Conrad

Kohrs, Alex Swan, Andrew Drumm, "Barbecue" Campbell, and scores of others will stand out as those of men of foresight and real vision who had the daring and the ability to try to make their dreams come true.

As for that most picturesque of all the sons of the Great West, the American cowboy, he has received far more voluminous treatment than have the cattlemen who were his employers. Yet, not many cowboys were really like the individual so often depicted on the screen or described in popular fiction. Two pictures of the cowpuncher are often drawn, both equally untrue. In some cases he is described as a kind of Sir Galahad, a knight without stain and a champion without reproach, who rode about over the prairies frequently rescuing blondes in distress and maybe occasionally doing a little work. In others he is depicted as a wild semi-outlaw, quick on the trigger, ready to fight at the drop of a hat and to drop it himself, a roistering, roaring hellion who spent most of his time in saloons consuming bad whisky and playing poker or other similar games with low and dissolute companions.

Both views fail to take into account the fact that cowpunching was a serious and exacting business requiring hard work, courage, and self-reliance. Ninety-five per cent of the cow hand's time, moreover, must be spent in regions equally remote from blondes, in distress or otherwise, and from the more or less bright lights of the festive cow towns. In consequence, little opportunity was afforded for playing either the hero or the villain even if he were so inclined, which in most cases he was not. That there were bad men and worthless men among the range riders cannot be denied, but their number was not large and even the worst were not as black as they have been painted, or as they at times sought to paint themselves. Cowboys were usually young men and youth is often boastful and inclined, even today, to exaggerate greatly its own tough and hard-boiled nature. Witness this proud boast of a Texas cow hand who was probably in reality a very ordinary and harmless individual.

> *I'm a buzzard from the Brazos on a tear;*
> *Hear me hoot.*
> *I'm a litter of the flowing locks of hair;*
> *Watch 'em scoot.*
> *I'm a coyote of the sunset, prairie dude;*
> *Hear me zip.*
> *In the company of gentlemen I am rude*
> *With my lip.*
> *Those who love me call me Little Dynamite;*
> *I'm a pet.*
> *I'm a walking, stalking terror of the night*
> *You can bet.*
> *With my nickle-plated teaser*
> *Many a rusty-featured greaser's*
> *Sun has set.*
> *Sometimes I strike an unprotected town,*
> *Paint it red,*
> *Choke the sheriff, turn the marshal upside down*
> *On his head.*
> *Call for drinks for all the party*
> *And if chinned by any smarty*
> *Pay in lead.*

Such a pose is humorous but, of course, does not describe anyone, least of all the man who penned the lines. A really bad man did not boast. He felt that actions spoke far louder than words.

The work of the range rider was of infinite variety yet at times was characterized by a deadly monotony. In its larger aspects it included driving trail herds, joining in the roundup, branding calves or selecting beef animals, and "riding a line," though there were also many other duties. Sometimes his work included breaking horses, hunting wolves, defense against cattle thieves, red or white, and the building of corrals or line camps. Naturally, he must do his own personal work, or those tasks necessary to enable him to live in reasonable comfort. For weeks at a time he must take care of his own camp, chop firewood, bring water from the spring, cook his meals, wash his clothing, bedding, and saddle blankets, and do the dozens of other little things that fall to the lot of one who lives alone. It is not strange that in time he developed a surprising degree of resourcefulness and the ability to take care of himself at all times and under all circumstances.

Among the major types of work of the cow hand, the driving of cattle on the trail bulked large. This included not only the long drives previously discussed, extending from Texas to the Kansas "cow towns" or to northern ranges, but also shorter ones moving cattle from one range to another, or the driving of a beef herd to some shipping point to be transported to market. The methods employed in these shorter drives did not differ essentially from those used in the longer ones from Texas, and the experiences of the riders were in both instances very much the same. In most cases driving cattle on the trail was at times characterized by great monotony, interspersed with occasional brief interludes of difficult and dangerous work when a swollen river must be forded or a stampede checked.

The roundups were perhaps less monotonous, but the

work was likely to be even harder. Often a huge territory must be covered, the cattle thrown together into large herds, and the calves cut out and branded, or the fat, mature animals ready for market thrown into the "beef herd," depending upon whether it was the spring or fall roundup. In the great roundups in which all the ranchmen of a large region participated, there might be many wagons and scores, or even hundreds, of men. Each rider had his "cutting horse" carefully trained for separating animals from a herd. Such a horse was a real treasure. With a flick of the end of a rope, the rider designated the animal to be driven from the herd and the intelligent cutting horse did the rest, requiring no guidance, but following the steer or calf with unerring precision until it had been thrown out of the herd and into the beef, or calf, herd held near by.

Though the roundup might involve much hard work, it also had its attractive features. The cooks vied with one another in preparing good food since each was eager to uphold the honor of the brand for which he worked. At night when the day's work was over, the men from the various outfits came together about the wagons and news was exchanged, jokes passed, and stories told. Often there was a considerable amount of rough horseplay but it was all in fun and was nearly always taken in that spirit. Anyone who found himself the victim of a practical joke usually merely sought to laugh it off and then to join in planning one on the next fellow.

Between roundups, or when not engaged in trail driving or some special duty, the range rider usually pursued the third major activity mentioned—that of "riding a line." As indicated in a previous essay, the boundaries of every ranchman's range were clearly defined by the common law of the range known as "cow custom." About its borders line camps were constructed at convenient sites and one or two riders placed at each of these, to ride the line and keep the cattle inclined to wander thrown back upon their own grazing grounds. By the early eighties the invention of barbed wire and its growing use by many ranchmen had resulted in the enclosure of many large areas by wire fencing. This by no means did away with the work of the line rider, though it was made somewhat easier. Yet the pasture fences must be ridden every day or two in order to keep them up and to see that animals did not break through. Fencing the public domain was forbidden by law, but so was the consumption of apples in the Garden of Eden!

Whether he was riding and keeping up a fence or merely riding the imaginary line which marked the border of his employer's range, the line rider's life was likely to be a lonely one. If two men were stationed at a camp it was not so bad, but in many cases a cow hand would be located all alone in a camp a great many miles from any other human habitation. He often saw no one for days and in exceptional cases for weeks at a time. Under such conditions he of course had a large measure of independence. He was for the time strictly his own boss, but his duties were many and varied. He must ride his line and keep up the fence or strive to keep the cattle on their own side of the line. Water holes must be visited and any helpless animal bogged down pulled from the mud by the rope attached to the saddle horn. Cattle must be protected from the depredations of wolves, white thieves, or Indians who, after the buffalo were gone, found in the white man's cattle a natural substitute. Any animal that had received a scratch or minor wound was, in summer, likely to be attacked by screw worms. Such animals must be roped, thrown, and the wound dressed with some kind of "worm medicine" which would destroy the parasites.

The camp itself usually consisted of a one-room dugout or half dugout with the door at one end and a fireplace for heat and cooking at the other. This must be kept clean and in order. Contrary to popular opinion the cowboy's camp was seldom dirty and disorderly. In some cases a line rider was as careful as the most meticulous housewife in the matter of housekeeping. With an improvised broom made of a large bunch of tall grass tied to a stick, the earthen floor was swept until it was entirely clean. The tin plates, cups, and pans were washed and polished until they shone like new silver. On the bedstead made of poles or rough lumber was placed a "straw tick" filled with dry prairie grass. This covered with blankets made an excellent bed. A table was made of the boards from old boxes and chairs or stools from willows or empty wire spools.

Whether the range rider were in camp, on the trail, or engaged in the roundup, his food was usually plentiful and good, though sometimes coarse and lacking in variety. Sourdough biscuits baked in a Dutch oven are, when made by an expert, unsurpassed by any other form of bread. On the roundup it was customary to kill a beef every day or two if a large number of men were to be fed, while the line rider usually had a quarter of beef hanging from the end of the ridge pole of the dugout or from the convenient branch of a tree. Bacon and beans were, of course, staple articles of diet, as were dried apples, peaches, or apricots. Rice, syrup, and at times canned corn or tomatoes were much in evidence.

With beef in abundance, broiled steak seldom figured in

the line rider's dietary scheme of things. Steak was fried in a little hot suet, or the meat was sometimes roasted in the Dutch oven or boiled in an iron pot over the fireplace and dumplings of biscuit dough added. Some outfits were famous for the way in which they fed their men and others notorious for the way they did not, but on the whole the average cowpuncher fared very well.

To the standard food supplies brought out every month or two by a wagon from headquarters, the line rider like the trail-drive cook frequently added some native products. He would catch a string of fish from a near-by stream, shoot some quail or wild turkeys, or gather dewberries, wild plums, grapes, and pecans in season. Sometimes an ambitious young man would in somewhat shamefaced fashion try his hand at making a pie, cake, or doughnuts. This was unusual, however. In most cases "slumgullion," a kind of bread pudding made from cold biscuits, sugar, and raisins marked the limit of his culinary imagination. More "fancy fixin's" were left to the nester's wife.

The hospitality of the Cow Country was boundless. Any stray rider who appeared at a line camp was not only invited but urged to stop and spend the night, and no questions asked. He might be either a wandering cow hand or an outlaw with a price on his head, but neither mattered. It was enough that he was hungry and needed shelter. He was welcome and the line rider was glad for his company. If he stopped at a camp and found no one there, he was at entire liberty to go in, cook himself a meal, and ride on after he had washed the dishes. On this last point the etiquette of the range spoke in no uncertain terms. Only a bum would cook and eat and then ride on leaving the dishes to be washed by his absent host.

Some men out of a job for the winter would merely ride from camp to camp throughout a wide area spending a night or so at each. This was commonly called "riding the chuck line," but such visitors were always gladly received. It was a part of the custom of the country. At the headquarters ranch it was the same. Strangers dropped in there at times to stay a day or a week, leaving only when the spirit moved them.

In spite of the monotony of trail driving, the strenuous labor of the roundups, and the loneliness of a remote line camp, cowboy life was not without its compensations. Every range rider loved his work, was proud of his job, and maintained an intense loyalty toward his employer and the brand.

There were exceptions, of course, but as a rule the range rider was shy, quiet, and soft spoken. In a region and a society where it is customary to go armed, courtesy is likely to be the rule. Armament, whether on the part of nations or individuals, seems to inspire courtesy and respect on the part of the neighbors.

The traditional weapon of the cowboy was the .45 caliber Colt's revolver, commonly called a "forty-five." It was usually carried either in a "Texas shoulder scabbard" just in front of the left arm, or in a holster on the hip. It was heavy and contrary to screen and fiction few men carried more than one, and even this was laid aside when engaged in the strenuous work of branding or cutting out cattle. Also, contrary to general opinion, few range riders were unusually skillful in its use. There were exceptions, of course, but the average cow hand was only a fair marksman with a pistol. The expert gunmen were more likely to be the frontier peace officers. Yet, the cowboy recognized the fact that a gun is the one unanswerable argument and usually wore his forty-five regularly, sometimes adding a Winchester rifle in a leather scabbard strapped to his saddle when riding a range infested with wolves or cattle thieves. Even though he might never need it the comforting pressure of the heavy forty-five against his body was very reassuring. As one cow hand put it:

> *When I recall that strange wild land,*
> *The long, lone nights for weeks on end*
> *When feeling you beneath my hand*
> *Was like the hand grip of a friend,*
> *For all your faults I can't contrive*
> *To cuss you—good old forty-five.*

Another myth with respect to the cowboy is that he delighted in riding wild and vicious horses. It is true that he often had to ride such animals and was even proud of his ability to do so if necessary, but to say that he liked it would be to brand the range rider as a near moron. A horse that bucks and uses his best efforts, every time he is saddled, to throw or kill the rider is an unmitigated nuisance. A bucking, bawling, sunfishing mount interferes both with the most efficient work and the pleasure to be derived from a ride to town or to visit friends. A gentle, well-broken horse was far more desirable though it must be confessed that the term "gentle and well broken" is a relative one capable of a good many interpretations.

The range rider's social diversions were naturally few and far between. At the end of a long drive he might spend a few days in the cow town, or occasionally accompany a trainload of cattle to Chicago, Kansas City, or one of the other markets. This and infrequent visits to some small frontier village constituted about his only contacts with town life. If at such times he sought to celebrate by taking a few drinks or joining in a game of poker, it was perhaps only natural. The idea that all or most cowboys became drunken, noisy rowdies as soon as they reached town, however, is entirely wrong. Some of them neither drank nor gambled at all, and the number that did either to excess was not great.

Yet, the cowboy's willingness to "try most anything once" and his readiness to resent what he regarded as an affront or unfair treatment frequently got him into scrapes and sometimes into jail, though most of his misdeeds were merely boyish pranks not in any sense due to a vicious nature or any evil intention.

"Do you think some fellows are just naturally unlucky?" an ill-featured cowhand called Slim once asked the author. "Well, *I* do," he continued without waiting for a reply. "I used to have a chum named Bill, that was that way. If anything happened to anybody, it allus happened to Bill. If somebody got stung by a wasp, or had his horse fall and stove him up, or got skinned up in a stampede, it was allus shore to be Bill. One evenin' Bill and another chum named Jim and me wuz in town and we wuz drinkin' a little—not much but just enjoyin' ourselves. It wuz a little bitty town— just one street with a few stores and saloons and a blacksmith shop. Down at the end of the street wuz an old vacant store building with a wooden porch in front of it and that day th' local judge was down there a-holdin' court. The sheriff was there too and a jury and all the fellers that uz bein' tried, and their witnesses, and of course a bunch of loafers. After while th' sheriff broke away and come up to th' saloon where we wuz and says to us: 'You fellers has got to git out o' town. You're drinkin' and the first thing you know you'll be drunk an' disorderly, and I'll have to slap you in jail. Git on your hosses now and git goin'.' I says, 'All right, we're goin' purty soon,' and he says, 'You're not goin' purty soon, you're goin' right now.' So we started out to git our hosses and he went back to wait on the court some more.

"We fiddled around a little gettin' our hosses and when we seen him disappear in the courtroom, decided we'd go back and have another drink and git some cigars. So in a few minutes he come back up to th' saloon and arrested all three of us and took us down to court and th' judge fined us five dollars apiece for bein' drunk and disorderly. Then he turned right around and fined Bill ten dollars more for contempt of court. Unlucky old Bill! Why all he was doin' was that he was sittin' there in a chair and ever' once in awhile he'd reach his foot out and drag his spur along over the floor.

"Purty soon th' judge says, 'quit that, will you? You're disturbin' th' court.' I guess Bill must a-forgot for in about a minute or so he done it agin and th' judge says: 'Ten dollars fer contempt of court. I told you once to quit that.' Well, we paid our fines and Bill's ten extry and went out and got on our hosses and then we decided that since we'd paid fer it we'd show our contempt fer th' court, judge, jury, sheriff, and everybody else in there by ridin' acrost that porch in front of th' court room as we went out o' town. So's we started down th' street in a high lope, Jim first, me next, and Bill last. Jim clattered acrost th' porch that had two or three loose boards, makin' an awful racket, and I clattered acrost right behind him. But do you know, Bill's hoss wasn't shod in front and fell flat right on that porch, and the sheriff, and judge, and jury all run out and caught him. They dragged him inside and fined him twenty-five dollars more, and he didn't have it, so they locked him up in jail and kep' him there four or five days till we could git up th' money and send somebody in to pay him out. We uz afraid to go back ourselves. You know, I think some fellers are just naturally *unlucky!*"

Visits to town were not frequent, however, so most of the range rider's fun or recreation must be sought on the prairie in connection with his work. In a man's country his opportunities for association with women were few and far between. Occasionally a dance might be held at the home of some ranchman whose wife and daughters had been willing to brave the hardships of frontier life, but such affairs were infrequent and men often outnumbered the girls ten to one.

Nearly every cow camp had a few books or magazines and these were usually read and reread until their contents had been pretty well memorized before an opportunity came to replenish the supply or exchange them for others. Such books were likely to be anything from hair-raising dime novels or sickly, sentimental love stories to Shakespeare, *Paradise Lost*, or Dante's *Divine Comedy*. Yet the range rider read them all diligently. One cow hand to whom the author had loaned a copy of the English poet Bailey's *Festus* brought it back some weeks later with the remark that there was "an awful lot of mighty good readin' in that book." Generous in this as in all other matters the cowboys would freely lend any books which they might have, with the result that some volumes circulated throughout a wide area.

An occasional cow hand played the violin, guitar, or banjo and nearly all were accustomed to singing, not only when standing guard at night, but in many cases merely while riding the range or working about camp. In many cases if a stray rider dropped into camp to spend the night, he and his host would sing for one another's entertainment until far into the night. Often if one of them sang a song which the other did not know but particularly liked, the latter would give the singer a pencil and piece of paper and ask him to "write the ballad," meaning the words, for the listener. He would then be requested to sing it again so that his hearer might become familiar with the tune. In this fashion a rider added to his store of songs from time to time.

Some men were widely known because of their excellent voices and a rich and varied repertoire of good songs. Such individuals were doubly welcome at any ranch house, line camp, or roundup wagon throughout an enormous region. Year by year their fame as entertainers became more widespread. They were troubadours of the Cow Country, minnesingers, or wandering minstrels, and their songs were of wide variety.

Cowboy songs seem to have become increasingly popular in recent years, but most of those sung on the range did not sound much like the ones commonly heard over the radio. Some were, of course, of the Rabelaisian type entirely unprintable, but the great majority were deeply romantic love songs that fairly dripped sentiment in every stanza. Many referred to the tragic death of some lovely sweetheart and the heartbroken yearnings of the bereaved lover, as in this one:

> *Thou wilt come no more, gentle Annie,*
> *Like a flower thy spirit did depart*
> *Thou hast gone, alas, like the many*
> *That have bloomed in the summer of my heart.*

> *Shall I never more behold thee,*
> *Never hear thy winning voice again,*
> *When the springtime comes, gentle Annie*
> *And the wild flowers lie scattered o'er the plain.*

In another, very popular among the range riders, the listener is requested to:

> *Close the brown eyes gently,*
> *Beautiful Mabel Clare,*
> *For no more shall I gather wild flowers*
> *To braid in your shining hair.*

In still another it is stated that

> *When the birds were a-singing in the morning,*
> *When the myrtle and the ivy were in bloom,*
> *When the sun o'er the hilltop was a-dawning,*
> *'Twas then we laid her in the tomb.*

All of these, together with such sentimental ballads as "Sadie Ray," "Too Late," "Faded Flowers," and a host of others, apparently originated somewhere in the East and were brought West to form a sort of link binding the Cow Country to the life of a more settled and civilized region.

Many others, however, more closely related to the range rider's life and work grew, like the buffalo grass or prickly pear, from the soil of the western plains. They, too, were of many types but, like the first named class, were often of a plaintive, mournful character. They included such favorites as "Bury Me Not on the Lone Prairie," "The Dying Cowboy," "The Dying Ranger," or the "Dying Californian," and were usually rendered with a quavering pathos that would wring the heart of a wooden Indian! They often had an unbelievably large number of stanzas suggesting that the hero must have died a long and lingering death. Surely if it took him as long to die as it did for the singer to reach the end of the ballad, his suffering must have been terrible!

These are usually regarded as the most typical of all cowboy songs, but there were others far different. There were the light, lilting ones with words to match:

> *I'll sell my horse*
> *And I'll sell my saddle*
> *And I'll bid farewell*
> *To th' long-horned cattle,*
> *And it's ti yi yoopy, yoopy*
> *Ti yi yay,*
> *And its ti yi yoopy yoopy yay.*

Or, to give another example:

> *Twas in the fall of '71*
> *I thought I'd see how*
> *Cowpunchin' was done.*
> *The boss said cowpunchin' was only fun,*
> *There wasn't a bit of work to be done,*
> *All you had to do was just to ride*
> *And go a-driftin' with the tide;*
> *The son-of-a gun, Oh how he lied*
> *In '71.*

Then there was the type in which love formed the theme, as: "Remember the Red River Valley and the Cowboy That

Loved You So True," or sometimes a deeply religious note
crept in, as in this:

> *Last night as I lay on the prairie*
> *Looking up at the stars in the sky,*
> *I wondered if ever a cowboy*
> *Could go to that sweet bye and bye.*
> *I wondered if ever a cowboy*
> *Could go to that sweet bye and bye.*
>
> *Someday there will be a grand roundup,*
> *Where cowboys like cattle will stand*
> *To be cut out by the Riders of Judgment*
> *Who are posted and know every brand.*
> *To be cut out by the Riders of Judgment*
> *Who are posted and know every brand.*
>
> *The road which leads down to perdition*
> *Is posted and blazed all the way,*
> *But the pathway which leads up to Heaven*
> *Is narrow and dim, so they say.*
>
> *Whose fault is it then that so many*
> *Go out on that wide range and fail*
> *Who might have honor and plenty*
> *Had they known of that dim, narrow trail?*

Such songs reveal the very heart and soul of the range
rider. He was lighthearted and frivolous at times, and at
others, very serious. He was often lonely. His respect for
pure womanhood amounting to something akin to reverence is too well known to require comment. He was at

heart deeply religious. He had seen men die with their boots on in very unpleasant fashion at times, and the thought of death and the world beyond grows strangely familiar when one lives close to it for a long time. These songs reflect his changing moods, his manner of thought, his way of life.

Some riders formulated tunes as well as words. They added new stanzas, thus extending the songs to remarkable lengths, improvised, and constructed parodies on the then popular songs of the day.

Other songs common to the Cow Country dealt with the lives and exploits of certain individuals who had lived without the law but had possessed certain personal characteristics which the range riders admired. One which was widely sung relates that:

> *Jesse left a wife*
> *To mourn all her life;*
> *Three children, they were brave,*
> *But a dirty little coward*
> *Shot Mr. Howard*
> *And laid Jesse James in his grave.*

Another almost as well known dealt with the life and death of Sam Bass:

> *Sam Bass was born in Indiana,*
> *It was his native home;*
> *And at the age of seventeen*
> *Young Sam began to roam.*
> *He first came out to Texas*
> *A teamster for to be;*
> *A kinder hearted fellow*
> *You seldom ever see.*

After going on through many stanzas to relate the story of Sam's life of how he "used to deal in race stock, one called the Denton mare," of his going up the trail to Dakota with a herd of Texas cattle and robbing the Union Pacific express train on the way back, the ballad eventually gets down to his tragic death at Round Rock, Texas. It concludes with a bitter denunciation of Sam's companion and false friend, Jim Murphy, who betrayed him to the Texas officers, stating that:

> *He gave poor Sam away*
> *And left his friends to mourn,*
> *And what a scorchin' Jim will get*
> *When Gabriel blows his horn.*

It is significant that nothing is said about the possibility of Sam's coming in for a bit of "scorching" in the next world despite his many crimes and that the author of the first song apparently shows some sympathy for the redoubtable Jesse James, or at least for his wife and children. The authors and singers of both songs doubtless did not condone the evil deeds of Sam and Jesse but felt that their crimes of robbing trains and banks always at the risk of their own lives rather paled into insignificance when compared with the far greater ones of shooting a companion in the back, or betraying to his death a trusting friend.

The terrible winter of 1886–87 followed by the rapid influx of settlers to the western prairies brought great changes to the Cow Country and to the range rider's life and work. The long drives from Texas slackened and eventually ceased entirely. The ranches grew smaller as the range area was reduced by the coming of the homesteaders. Fenced pastures, well-bred cattle, and winter feeding became the rule. But though the work of the cowboy was changed and many were compelled to give up their chosen vocation, the cowboy himself remained essentially the same. Not a few old-time range riders may still be found within the limits of the onetime Cow Country. Here in an environment that must be to them forever strange they still retain in the midst of an unfamiliar social and economic order their old-time ideals and state of mind. The conditions which produced them have long ago gone forever, but they still persist and will remain with the cow hands so long as they shall live, as a deathless heritage from the past.

For it would seem that the man who rode the range for many years unconsciously developed a somewhat intangible philosophy of life. Perhaps his point of view and his heart and soul came to partake of the nature of the wide plains that were the field of his work causing him to despise everything small, petty, and mean whether in thought, or word, or deed. Whatever vices he might have were large ones and his virtues even larger. To explain this philosophy of life is difficult. Perhaps it is best summed up in these verses written by Badger Clark, a real cowboy of the old school, in *Sun and Saddle Leather:*

> *O Lord, I've never lived where churches grow;*
> *I've loved creation better as it stood*
> *That day you finished it, so long ago,*
> *And looked upon your work and called it good.*
>
> *I know that others find you in the light*
> *That's sifted down through tinted windowpanes,*
> *And yet I seem to feel you near tonight*
> *In the dim, quiet starlight of the plains.*

Just let me live my life as I've begun!
  And give me work that's open to the sky;
Make me a partner of the wind and sun,
  And I won't ask a life that's soft and high.

Make me as big and open as the plains;
  As honest as the horse between my knees;
Clean as the wind that blows behind the rains;
  Free as the hawk that circles down the breeze.

Just keep an eye on all that's done and said;
  Just right me sometime when I turn aside;
And guide me on the long, dim trail ahead—
  That stretches upward towards the Great Divide.

VII

The Humor of the Cowboy

We never failed to laugh at every danger,
For laughter we accounted not a sin;
And any time there came to us a stranger
Who seemed a trifle fresh, we took him in.
We regaled his ears with every fearful story
That occurred to us and there were quite a few;
And we didn't hesitate on details gory
But manufactured many that were new.
And yet there was some method in our madness,
Such hazing was according to a plan;
For we welcomed him to brotherhood with gladness
If the tenderfoot should prove himself a man.

COWHANDS AND TENDERFEET

WHETHER OR NOT THERE IS ANY such thing as a distinctive cowboy humor may well be open to question. Perhaps what is so called is merely a phase of that robust humor of the Great West as a whole expressed in the pungent vernacular of the range country and reflecting the cowboy's psychology as developed by his vocation and daily life. Some understanding of that psychology, some knowledge of the cowboy himself, his way of life, and habits of thought would appear necessary in order to understand and appreciate fully his humorous utterances.

As has been indicated in an earlier essay, the cowboy was neither a shining knight of the type adorning the pages of romantic novels with a medieval setting, nor a near outlaw. He was a man of action—a young man in most cases—who rode hard, frequently swore hard, lived according to his code, and who, with few exceptions, showed at all times loyalty and sincere devotion to the interests of his employer. "Just folks! Just plain, ordinary, bowlegged humans—that's cowpunchers," said an old range rider who knew all too well whereof he spoke.

Yet the cowboy was in his own eyes at least something of an aristocrat and the world has been inclined to accept him at his own valuation, for in all ages the man who rides, whether he be called cavalier, *Ritter*, *caballero*, knight, or cowpuncher, has regarded himself as superior to the man who walks and ever there has clustered about him some of the romantic glamour always associated with the man on horseback.

Perhaps the most pronounced characteristic of the cow hand in common with that of most other Westerners was his tendency to tell tall stories. The writer, while a student at Harvard, ate at a table in Memorial Hall with a group of men from the Southwest—mostly from the range area of Texas. Toward midyear a young New Englander who had been graduated from Amherst asked permission to eat at our table. At the end of three or four weeks he remarked, "You men are all fine fellows, and I like you very much, but I'm afraid I'll never understand your peculiar sense of humor. You start in and lie in most remarkable fashion and seem to think it's funny. I just can't understand it."

The bewilderment of the young New Englander was probably due to the fact that at dinner the evening before some of the men were describing the wonders of their old home state of Texas. One declared that in the region where he lived along the Pecos the soil was so rich that it was impossible to raise watermelons. The vines grew so fast that they dragged the little melons along over the ground and just naturally wore them out!

Another asserted that in his neighborhood in the valley of the Brazos nobody ever thought of planting corn. One man had once accidentally dropped a kernel near the back door which came up and grew with amazing rapidity. His little boy went out one day and started to climb up the stalk, but when he had gone up some distance and tried to climb down again the stalk was growing so rapidly that he kept getting farther and farther from the ground all the time. His father hearing his screams ran out with an axe and tried to chop the stalk down, but though the axe bit deep into the soft wood at every blow, the gash made was up out of reach before a second blow could be struck. He said the pitiful cries of the youngster nearly broke his father's heart. His parents never saw him again and judged that he finally starved to death and his body must have lodged among the giant leaves. He undoubtedly lived for some time on raw corn, however, for though he was much too far away for them to hear longer his piteous cries, the cobs kept falling for more than three weeks! Some weeks later the father died. When he reached Heaven, he eagerly inquired of St. Peter about his son.

"Your son is not here," said the Keeper of the Pearly Gates. "At least I don't think he is."

"He must be," insisted the father. "He was always a good boy. About six weeks ago he went out into the backyard to climb a cornstalk and disappeared in the clouds and never came back."

"Oh yes," said Saint Peter. "I remember now that a boy did pass through here on a cornstalk a few weeks ago, but he was going so fast we couldn't stop him!"

Another chap, shifting the conversation somewhat, said that in his neighborhood out near Amarillo the people always put bells on their children to keep the hawks from carrying them off and that he himself had once shot a hawk with a wing spread of a little over fifty feet. To this he got no response except from a young fellow from El Paso who remarked:

"Gosh! It must have been a young 'un."

Such wild yarns are the natural product of the Cow Country, for the cowpuncher even though he was seldom a talkative individual when he did speak was often as extravagant in his statements as he was with his money and that was in all conscience extravagant enough! "I had fifty dollars only last night," said Buck Winters, "and this mornin' I ain't got a cent!" "What happened to it?" someone asked.

"Well, I went to town and drifted into a saloon and asked everybody to have a drink and a bite to eat. That cost me ten dollars. Then I went up the street a piece and went into another saloon and invited everybody to drink and eat. That cost another ten dollars. Then I crossed over the street to another saloon and had 'em all drink an' eat and that cost fifteen dollars. So I ain't got a cent this mornin'."

"But that's only thirty-five dollars," said someone. "Ten and ten and fifteen make thirty-five and you said you had fifty. What did you do with the other fifteen dollars?"

Buck scratched his head, "I don't know boys. By that time I uz gettin' pretty drunk. I'm afraid I must have spent that other fifteen dollars foolishly!"

Fairly typical of the tall tales of the range country is the old yarn of the mountain-lion driver. It is said that some years ago the usual Saturday afternoon crowd of loafers was gathered about a crossroads store in western Arkansas. Looking up the road toward the west, they saw a little cloud of dust approaching and as it came nearer they saw a most astonishing spectacle—a man in a two-wheeled cart to which was hitched a pair of mountain lions. The man himself was an unkempt, bearded individual with two six-shooters buckled about his waist and a bowie knife in his belt. A huge wild cat with a spiked collar about its neck sat on the seat beside him and the man was driving his fearsome team with a live rattlesnake for a whip. He pulled up in front of the store with a loud *Whoa!* laid down his rattlesnake, and asked:

"Has anybody here got anything to drink?" There was a moment's silence and then one man diffidently stated that he had a little corn whisky.

"Corn whisky is no sort of a drink for a *man*," roared the newcomer, "ain't you got no sulphuric acid?" After another pause someone remarked that there was some in the store.

"Bring me a quart of it," cried the newcomer. It was brought and, draining the liquid at a few gulps, the visitor picked up his rattlesnake, gathered up the lines and said:

"Well, cats, we've got to be goin'. Much obleeged, men."

Then one of the goggle-eyed crowd summoned up courage to ask:

"Stranger, whare be ye frum? We ain't seen anybody like you in these parts afore. Whare do you live at anyhow?"

"I'm frum Oklahomy," said the stranger. "To tell you th' truth, men, th' damned Ku Klux is gettin' so bad out there it's runnin' all of us sissies out."

The cowboy delights in such wild stories and his speech is filled with fantastic exaggerations:

"Take that steak back to th' kitchen and have 'em cook it some more," yelled Sam Williams to a waiter. "Why I've seen 'em git well that uz hurt worse'n that!"

This brings to mind one of the oldest of all cowboy stories—that of Hank Blevins who, reaching Kansas City with a trainload of cattle, repaired to a swell restaurant for dinner. At the next table a girl and two men were giving their orders:

"Waiter," said the girl, "I want a thick steak, a rare steak please."

"Bring me a steak too," said one of the men, "and I want mine very rare."

"I'll have a steak myself," said the next man, "but I want it extremely rare. Just sear the outside a little."

"Waiter," said Hank, when it came his turn, "just cripple him and drive him in. I'll eat him."

Next to telling wildly impossible stories or making super-exaggerated statements, the cowboy's sense of humor perhaps most often found expression in what he would call "stringing the tenderfoot," particularly if the latter were inclined to be either "fresh" or overfastidious.

"He was a stranger and I took him in," was the cow hand's favorite text. If the newcomer prepared to sleep on the ground, he was warned of rattlesnakes and told to lie perfectly quiet without moving a muscle if he felt one crawling into his bed, for in no other way could he hope to avoid being bitten. If he fitted up a cot he was urged to beware of the deadly centipedes which were always seeking to climb up on something in order to get off the cold ground. If he wished to sleep in the chuck wagon, mention was made of the horrible "pohelia monster," far more poisonous than the rattler, and which had a peculiar affinity for wagons and could climb a wagon wheel as quickly as the tree lizard runs up a tree. The cry of a little screech owl or night hawk reaching the ears of the tender-foot and a few old cow hands as they sat about a camp-fire was interpreted as the bloodcurdling scream of the awful *walli galoo*, a cross between a panther and a grizzly bear and far more dangerous than either. Heads were solemnly shaken and grave doubts expressed as to whether from one to three of the little group would not in all probability be carried off and eaten before morning!

The harmless old Indian smoking a cigarette in front of the trading post was pointed out as a blood-thirsty old warrior who boasted that he had ninety-nine scalps with varying colors of hair and that he was determined before he died to round out his collection with one more bearing hair of exactly the shade of that of the open-mouthed and horror stricken listener. He was taken on snipe hunts and was induced to creep up under the cover of darkness to view Indian war dances in which painted and befeathered cowpunchers in red blankets cavorted about a campfire and with fearful war whoops charged the hidden spectators at exactly the right moment. He was served fried skunk alleged to be rabbit and ate it ravenously while his companions looked on with eyes that registered envy as they mournfully expressed their regret that rabbit disagreed with them.

He was given the sleepy looking outlaw horse to ride and was regaled with horrid tales of the dangers from venomous tarantulas, hydrophobia cows, and from the river quicksands, which could suck down horse and rider in the twinkling of an eye. If he showed himself a good sport he was eventually regarded as initiated and admitted to the charmed circle, but woe to the luckless individual who failed to take such hazing in good sport, or who manifested weakness and irritation.

The cowboy frequently indulged in short, pithy sayings that might be designated as "wise cracks." Some of these are not only humorous but show as well an unconscious philosophy:

"You've got to handle a lot of people just like mules," Johnnie Hawkins once said. "Don't try to drive 'em into a corral. Just leave the corral gate unhooked and a little bit open and let 'em bust in."

"Talkin' about music," remarked a later time cowpuncher, "I used to own a saxophone, but traded it off for a cow. Made about the same noise and gave milk besides."

"Guess I'll have some soup," said Bud Hilton to the waiter.

"All we've got is ox-tail soup, Sir."

"Well, let it go and bring me some ham an' eggs," answered Bud. "That's too far to go back for soup."

Jim Collins, of the Half Circle H, once went to a wedding in company with one of his chums. The bride was the blooming daughter of an old nester and the groom an impecunious and shiftless granger kid. When they reached that stage of the ceremony where the bridegroom said, "With all my worldly goods I thee endow," Jim nudged his companion and spoke in a stage whisper: "There goes Sam's shot gun. Somebody stole his dog just last week."

"This letter is from my old partner, Bill, down at San Antone," said a young cow hand. "Bill is a nice chap, but an awful ignorant feller. Just look. Here he spells Jesus with a little g."

Uncle Ike Hubbard was once eating supper at the round-up wagon and at the same time complaining about the grub. Finally the cook got so sore that he became quite sarcastic:

"Do you think you kin manage to eat the biscuits, Uncle Ike," said he with strained sweetness, "or shall I throw 'em out and try makin' up another batch?"

"They haint so bad," answered Uncle Ike. "If you put a lot o' this butter on 'em you can't taste 'em quite so much. Course you kin taste th' butter, but then I'm purty strong myself, as the feller said, and anyhow your coffee's weak enough to bring up th' general average."

An old bachelor ranchman in West Texas who owned a couple of million dollars worth of land and cattle had a sister who had married a successful businessman in Chicago. She wrote her brother, urging that he come and visit her for two or three days the next time he shipped cattle to Chicago, saying that she had a girl picked out for him. He came and a little party was arranged with dinner at a downtown hotel and a show afterward. The lady whom the sister had chosen for him was of the gushing type and the old cowman did not like her. After dinner it was decided to walk the three or four blocks to the theater. As they went out the door the old rancher managed surreptitiously to slip a chew of tobacco into his mouth and he and the girl trailed along a few feet behind the sister and her husband. The girl chattered incessantly and at last said, "Oh, I suppose you must own a great many cattle, don't you Mistah Johnson?" The old ranchman shifted his tobacco to the other side of his mouth, as expertly as a modern driver shifts gears, and replied solemnly:

"No ma'm, I don't reely own any cattle at all myself, but I'm cookin' fer one of the biggest outfits in West Texas." He said his companion refused to say another word all evening and that this marked the end of her beautiful friendship with his sister.

Andy Adams in his *Log of a Cowboy* relates that a cowpuncher became half drunk at a dance one night. Presently he asked a girl to dance with him, but noticing his condition she refused, whereupon he promptly told her to "go to hell!" She reported to her brother and the latter angrily demanded that an apology be made. With some reluctance the intoxicated cow hand hunted her up and said: "Miss, I just wanted to tell you that after all you don't need to go to hell. Your brother an' me has made other arrangements."

Some years ago an investigation was under way relative

to a most destructive train wreck that had occurred out in the southwest range country. Two trains had crashed together in a frightful head-on collision at a blind curve where the railway swept around the point of a long, high ridge. Most of the members of both train crews had been killed or injured, but the investigators at last found an old ranchman who had witnessed the disaster.

"Tell us exactly what you saw," demanded the chairman of the investigating committee. "Well, I was ridin' along the backbone of that ridge lookin' for mavericks when I saw off down to the south a train comin' north about fifty miles an hour. Then I looked north an' saw another 'un comin' south at about the same speed and I saw they uz goin' to smash into one another right at that curve."

"What did you do?" asked the chairman.

"Do? I didn't do nothin'."

"Didn't you ride down there and try to stop 'em?"

"No."

"Didn't you even *think* anything?"

"Yes, I thought a little."

"What did you think?"

"Well, I thought to myself that's a helluva way to run a railroad."

Contrary to popular opinion, obscenity was by no means the kernel to every cowboy jest. Some foul-spoken individuals were to be found, of course, but they were the exception and one can probably hear quite as many off-color stories around a college campus as circulated about the cow camp and roundup wagon. Profanity was common enough, but quite a number of range riders never swore and some even sought to discourage profanity on the part of others.

One well-known foreman was particularly diligent in

this respect and, visiting the line camp of two of his punchers, once made known his views at great length for the special benefit of one of the men named Cal McCoy, who was peculiarly gifted in the use of picturesque language. The foreman insisted that swearing was only a habit and that the quoting of Scripture would relieve one's feelings equally as well. Soon after he had left the next morning the two punchers decided to take the day off and do their quarterly washing. They stretched a line from the corner of the dugout to a near-by mesquite tree and after working hard over the tub all morning finally finished and set to work to hang out their clothes to dry. Unfortunately, just as the last piece was hung the line broke and all the clean garments came down in the dirt. Cal lifted his eyes toward Heaven and solemnly murmured: "Blessed are the meek, for they shall inherit the earth."

The cowboy's reverence for pure womanhood is well known. One night Bill Jones and a small group of men had assembled in a general merchandise store which also housed the post office and were waiting for the mail to be put up. Presently a girl came in and stopped in a somewhat shadowy corner of the store to wait for the post-office window to be opened. The conversation died down until all at once the door was flung open and a half drunk cowpuncher lurched in. Not seeing the girl he called out a greeting liberally sprinkled with profanity. Bill acted promptly. He stepped quickly across the room, caught the newcomer by the throat, shook him violently, and said:

"*Blankety, blank, blank, blank.* I'd like for you to *blankety, blank, blank* well understand that no *blankety, blank, blank,* can use such language in the presence of a lady when *I'm* around." The interesting point of the incident is that the girl dimpled and smiled and seemed to regard Bill as a great hero.

Cowboy humor occasionally found expression in the form of verse. The author in company with two other men was once snowbound for three weeks in a remote cow camp seventy-five miles from a railroad. A heavy snow had fallen followed by sleet so that it was impossible to ride. The cattle were in good shape, however, and had access to many large haystacks so there was nothing to worry about except the problem of finding something to do during the long days and what seemed like even longer winter evenings. The mornings were spent in tramping over the snow hunting and the afternoons and evenings in playing cards, checkers, or dominoes. The two or three magazines were read and re-read, stories were told and jokes passed, and finally one evening when all else had failed one man proposed that a contest be held in writing what he called "poetry." The man scheduled to do the day's cooking had baked a large, dried-apple pie which naturally cuts into four pieces, and it was proposed that the winner be given the extra piece of pie. The suggestion was welcomed since it promised amusement and for the next hour deep silence reigned within the cabin while the three toiled with pencil and paper to produce something worthy of their best efforts. Then the alleged "poems" were read aloud and the prize awarded.

The first man based his verses upon his duck hunting expedition of some weeks before which had resulted in the expenditure of much powder and shot and yielded in return only one small mud duck. He wrote:

MY DUCK HUNT

At break of day one morning gray
With blunderbuss and little fuss
I left my bed and fondly said,
"I'll try my luck at shooting duck."
To a marsh near by with tan weeds high
I bent my steps through the weedy depths
And thought with a laugh how my better half
Would find when she waked fat ducks to be baked.
But alas for each plan of mouse and of man;
I shot all my loads, I silenced the toads,
I ran amuck as for teal and for duck
And found—ah then—I had killed a mud hen.

The second man based his production upon a well-known
steer of the Lazy Z brand that had an evil temper and had
once chased Bill Jones to a place of safety on the top of a
sod house and had kept him there in durance vile until some
of the boys had come out and driven the animal away. This
steer, known as "Old Spot," had disappeared some days later
and it was currently reported that Bill had killed him. The
verses were as follows:

Did you ever hear of the piebald steer
That belonged to the Lazy Z?
He looked more queer, that piebald steer,
Than any I ever did see.

He was black and white, he was sure a sight,
For he'd spots of red besides;
And his temper grim was the worst of him,
When he comes the wise man rides.

> *He chased Bill Jones over sticks and stones*
> *To a friendly sod house roof,*
> *From which safe perch Bill left the church*
> *And cussed him from horn to hoof.*
>
> *But our country's sons have weighty guns*
> *And Bill remembers well.*
> *So we all did fear that the piebald steer*
> *To earth must bid farewell.*
>
> *How he came to go we do not know*
> *But his old haunts know him not,*
> *And we all believe when he came to leave*
> *That Bill was on the spot.*
>
> *So drop a tear for the piebald steer*
> *Though Bill may guiltless be;*
> *But a spotted hide on his fence I spied*
> *With the brand of the Lazy Z.*

The third man had started to Kansas City with a shipment of cattle some months before and, when the train took the siding up in Kansas to let a passenger train pass, had gone up to a well to get a pail of water. Unfortunately his train had pulled out while he was gone and left him as he said "broke and afoot and a thousand miles from home." His verses were based on this incident and he called them for no apparent reason under the sun "Far, Far Away."

> *My friends, if you will hear my verse,*
> *I'll clear my troubled brain*
> *And tell you a tale of the red-haired curse*

Whose fate was bad though it might have been worse,
Who lost his evening train.

This red-haired curse was a cowboy gay
Far, far away.
And his train rolled into a town one day
Far, far away,
And the cowboy, seizing a wooden pail
And holding fast to its battered bail,
Says "water we'll have or go to jail"
Far, far away.

He went straight up to the public well
Far, far away,
And at once proceeded the bucket to fill
Far, far away.
Then he heard a whistle and then a shout
And turning his body round about
He saw his train just pulling out
Far, far away.

He struck a gait that was far from slow
Far, far away.
His hat blew off but he let it go
Far, far away.
He raised his voice in many a yell,
His wrath was greater than tongue could tell,
And he wished the water back in the well
Far, far away.

He dashed along with a royal will
Far, far away.
Till at last the train went over a hill
Far, far away.

Then he settled down to count the ties
And to the next town straightway hies,
With blood and thunder in his eyes,
But the train is gone and still she flies,
Far, far away.

Perhaps not many cowpunchers ever essayed strictly original verse, but not a few would sometimes write parodies on well-known poems. Witness this production from the pen of Bill Jones when his girl threw him over and began to accept the attentions of his friend, Tommy Smith:

How dear to my heart was old Johnson's plantation
In days past and gone when I visited there;
When I left every task in my loved occupation
To see fairest Mary with bright, golden hair.
But now, far removed from that loved situation,
From Mary and all of her kin and her kith,
My thoughts often turn with but scant approbation
To him who has won her, my friend Tommy Smith.
Oh that lean, lanky Tommy,
That naughty boy Tommy,
That softheaded Tommy,
Whose last name is Smith.

Upon an occasion Tommy Smith's horses had strayed away and he was forced to ride one of the mules from the chuck wagon when he went to call upon Mary. Bill learned that the lady had received her mule-riding knight errant a bit coldly, so promptly sent her this couplet.

Oh dearest Mary, what makes you so cruel
When I come to see you a-riding my mu-el.

Such absurd rhymes reveal the gay, boyish spirit of the old-time cowboy who was ever inclined to laugh at danger and to meet "the slings and arrows of outrageous fortune" with a smiling face and a careless, bantering phrase. It was a spirit characteristic of our frontiersmen as a whole, who always seemed to find a keen sense of humor the best defense against the hardships and trials of pioneer life. It would almost seem that it has become nationwide in scope, or an American trait which has come down to us as a part of our frontier heritage.

Part V

Regional Development

VIII

Ranching on the Cheyenne-Arapaho Reservation

I grazed my cows in the long ago
On the old Cheyenne and Arapaho;
The Agent John D. Miles each day
Worshiped his God in the Quaker way.
But who were the gods of most of that crew
God in his infinite wisdom knew.
Whirlwind, White Shield, wise old chief,
Always fond of the white man's beef;
Fenlon, Evans, and Hunter too,
Dickey Brothers and "Barbecue";
Amos Chapman, the old squaw man,
Wed to a wife of the wild Cheyenne;
Good John Seger, a patient saint,
Feathered warriors bedecked with paint;
Billy Malaley and Cheyenne Belle,
These were some that I knew quite well;
And many more in the long ago,
On the old Cheyenne and Arapaho.

THE CHEYENNE COUNTRY

BETWEEN 1880 AND 1885 A SERIES OF
events took place on the Cheyenne-Arapaho reservation
in Indian Territory which attracted nationwide attention
and had a far-reaching influence upon the range cattle industry of the United States. This reservation lay in the western part of the Territory just south of the Cherokee Outlet
and was bounded on the east by the Oklahoma Lands, on
the south by Greer County and the reservations of the
Kiowa-Comanche and Wichita Indians, and on the west by
the Panhandle of Texas.

The reservation embraced about 4,300,000 acres on which
lived about 3,500 Indians of whom approximately two-thirds
were Cheyenne and one-third Arapaho. It had been set aside
by executive order in 1869. The agency was located at Darlington near the southeast corner, not far from the military
post of Fort Reno. The agent in 1880 was John D. Miles,
who had been there since about 1872. He was an able and
efficient executive who had ruled wisely and well these fierce
tribesmen—at that time among the wildest and most intrac-
table Indians of the entire country.

Among the first cattle to enter this region were the herds
of beef contractors. Under the "reservation policy" adopted

by the United States government it was necessary to feed the Indians, especially after buffalo began to grow scarce because of the activity of the hide hunters. Contracts were accordingly made with ranchmen in Texas and elsewhere and beef herds were brought in and pastured on the reservation near the agency in order to supply the Indians with food.

Long before 1880 two well-defined trails had been developed across the reservation leading north to the Kansas "cow towns." One of these — the Chisholm Trail — cut through the eastern part of it not far from the agency, while the other, the Western Trail, crossed the south fork of Red River at Doan's Store and meandered northward across the prairie, passing through the western part of the reservation and on across the Cherokee Outlet past Fort Supply to Dodge City. The region was well grassed and had an abundant water supply, so men driving north from Texas over these trails frequently turned aside for days and weeks in order to fatten their cattle on the rich pasture lands and so deliver them in good condition at the markets.

By 1880, in addition to the herds of the beef contractors and these cattle nominally on the trail, cattle were drifting in from Greer County, Texas, or the Cherokee Outlet, or were being driven in by ranchmen operating along the border or in near-by Kansas. Some of these men sought a more or less permanent occupation of these lands with their cattle. Good range was growing scarce and it is quite natural that enterprising cattlemen should turn their attention to this inviting area. Among the men who sought to pasture cattle on the Cheyenne-Arapaho reservation quite early on a permanent or semipermanent basis were Dickey Brothers, whose range lay near the northern boundary and extended across it into the Cherokee Outlet, B. H. Campbell—better known as "Barbecue Campbell"—and a number of others. As the need for range grew more and more pressing others came in, so by 1882 a number of men were pasturing cattle on the reservation, probably in most cases under some kind of tentative arrangement made with a band of Indians but no doubt in other instances without any arrangement whatever.

These men fully recognized the precarious nature of their tenure, but whatever efforts they had made to place their business on a more certain footing had met with no success owing to the fact that the Department of the Interior claimed it had no right to grant leases of Indian lands for grazing purposes or to give permission to occupy them with cattle. As early as 1879, R. D. Hunter, who was at that time a beef contractor at the Kiowa-Comanche agency, had asked permission to place herds of cattle upon that reservation in consideration of the payment of ten cents a head per year but his request had been refused. The following year he had sought permission to occupy the Oklahoma Lands with cattle but had again met with refusal. Other requests came in thick and fast during the next year or two. Some of these were for permission to occupy Greer County with herds, others for the privilege of pasturing cattle upon some of the reservations or the Oklahoma Lands.

All of these were refused, but the Department of the Interior was far away and the need for range great. By 1882 the cattle business was in a most flourishing condition. Prices had begun to advance sharply in 1881 and by 1882 had reached a level never before equaled except for a brief period during the Civil War. As a result, when cattle were set in motion in the spring of that year new ranges were sought with a feverish eagerness. Even while the Secretary of the Interior was refusing his permission, cattle were pouring into Greer County in large numbers. Ikard and Harrold brought herds into that region in 1881 and by 1882 their cattle in Greer County numbered sixty thousand head. Some of these drifted across the North Fork of Red River onto the Kiowa-Comanche lands; others came onto this reservation across the south fork of Red River from Texas, and by February, 1882, the Secretary of the Interior was so alarmed by this influx of cattle that he called upon the War Department for aid in removing them.

The War Department responded in very half-hearted fashion since its officers in the field were most reluctant to undertake the task and asserted it could not be done with any degree of success. They insisted that this was work the army should not be called upon to do and declared that the Department of the Interior should allow grazing upon Indian lands in consideration of the payment of a fee for that privilege.

With this idea the agents in direct charge of the Indians fully agreed. They were having a difficult time feeding their charges and keeping them contented. The first beef contracts had been made at a time when the Indians could eke out their beef ration very considerably by hunting buffalo. In the late 70's, however, buffalo began to grow scarce, and by 1880 the southern herd had been virtually exterminated. Yet the beef issue was not increased in quantity and the Indians were often hungry and in consequence restive and ripe for trouble.

Early in 1882 Agent P. B. Hunt, of the Kiowa-Comanche reservation, was notified that owing to lack of funds it would be necessary to reduce the beef ration of his Indians one-third. Convinced that this could not be done without serious trouble and possibly bloodshed he determined to take the matter of grazing upon his reservation into his own hands without waiting for orders from Washington. He accordingly recalled his police who were assisting the military in the latter's somewhat feeble effort to remove cattle from the reservation and sent one of his subordinates to seek out the ranchmen who owned the trespassing cattle to propose that if they would make good the beef deficiency he would not disturb them until after July the first.

The ranchmen eagerly assented, and the arrangement was made. The order reducing the beef ration was later countermanded, however, so Hunt had the cattlemen give him breeding animals for the Indians instead of beef. What Hunt's superior officers thought of this arrangement is not apparent but it seems probable that they did not approve of his action though they made no direct protest. Several requests for grazing permits in the Indian Territory were refused, however, in the spring of 1882, and in the meantime the situation with respect to trespassing cattle grew steadily worse. Late in April a group of Wichita and Caddo Indians complained to the Commissioner of Indian Affairs that their lands, or lands claimed by them, were occupied by 150,000 head of cattle which were causing them great damage by destroying their best range and bringing disease among their own small herds.

This complaint was transmitted by the Commissioner to the Secretary of the Interior and the latter once more called upon the War Department for aid in removing all cattle from the Indian Territory except the Quapaw reservation where licenses to graze had been granted, the country of the Five Civilized Tribes, and the land along well-defined trails.

To this request the Secretary of War did not reply for

more than a month. At the end of that time he sent to the Secretary of the Interior a brief note calling attention to a number of enclosures in the form of letters from officers in the field. Most important of these was a long letter from General Pope, commanding the Department of the Missouri. In this letter Pope stated that there were three classes of cattle in the Indian Territory: those passing through on trails, cattle pastured on the lands of the Cherokee Outlet under an arrangement made between the cattlemen and the Cherokee Indians, and those that were in the Territory without any right whatever. He said that trail drivers frequently turned aside for days and weeks at a time or lingered along the trail itself fattening their cattle as they slowly advanced, and that the three classes of cattle were so hopelessly mixed that he deemed it impossible to separate them. He declared that he did not think the military should be called upon to do this work and while if ordered to remove trespassing cattle he should try to obey yet he had scant hope of success unless he had a much larger force at his disposal. He closed his letter with the statement that in his opinion all permits to graze cattle in the Indian Territory or to pass through it with herds should be revoked, the trails closed, and the drovers forced to go around the Indian country with their herds. Pope's letter was endorsed by General Sheridan with the statement that he entirely agreed with these views. Among the other enclosures were a number of letters from subordinate officers in the field all commenting upon the unsatisfactory nature of their experience in trying to do this work.

While the whole matter of grazing upon the lands of the Indian Territory was in this condition, Agent Miles, of the Cheyenne-Arapaho reservation, found himself facing a most embarrassing situation. The supply of beef for these Indians had been reduced by an order from Washington and they were hungry and began to threaten trouble. Miles accordingly wired the Commissioner of Indian Affairs to the effect that the Indians had assembled in council and requested that he be permitted to place a few herds of cattle upon remote parts of the reservation and collect a grazing tax in order to make good this beef deficiency as they could not subsist upon the present issue of eighty thousand pounds a week. This telegram was followed by a letter in which Miles explained that he had met and talked with a number of cattlemen and that the latter had assured him they would be glad to make up the deficiency in consideration of grazing privileges and that this could be done without interfering in any way with the Indians or encroaching upon the range of their own small herds of cattle and ponies. Miles said that it would require at least 126,000 pounds of beef a week to supply the Indians and that this much must be furnished regularly or there would surely be hunger, discontent, and acts of lawlessness. To this request of Miles, however, Commissioner Price returned a curt and peremptory refusal.

Apparently both Miles and the Indians were much disappointed at this refusal and the latter became so restive as to cause the military commander at Fort Reno only two or three miles from the agency great uneasiness. That officer accordingly telegraphed General Pope that trouble was threatening, and if the Commissioner of Indian Affairs would heed Agent Miles' recommendation and allow grazing on the reservation, the beef deficiency could readily be made up and the Indians satisfied. He said that if such trouble did occur because of reduced rations the Indian Bureau should be held entirely responsible. General Pope transmitted this communication to his division commander with the endorsement that he saw no possible objection to permitting grazing on the lands of the Cheyenne-Arapaho reservation in consideration of the payment of a fair price and that he hoped the Commissioner of Indian Affairs would reconsider his action. He said that in this case it would cure a trouble that might soon be past dealing with except by war and urged that enough grazing be permitted to allow the Indians their full supply of beef. The Division Commander, General Sheridan, forwarded these communications to the Secretary of War and they eventually found their way to the Department of the Interior.

Commissioner Price was furious when these documents reached him and indignantly asserted that he took his orders from the Department of the Interior and not the Department of War. He declared that he did not propose to change his policy because of threats and unfavorable comments of others and said that if war had been averted thus far it had not been due to the payment of money for grazing since none had been paid. He clearly resented deeply what he felt was an unwarranted attempt of the military to influence his policy.

Fortunately the threatened trouble did not come. It seems probable, however, that a part of the beef deficiency was made up by trespassing cattlemen on the reservation either with the knowledge and consent of Agent Miles or with his tacit approval and that the Indians made up the remainder for themselves by preying upon any cattle within reach or by levying tribute upon herds on the trail. Miles reported that he had asked the troops at Fort Reno to remove trespassing cattle after August 19, but since there was only an imaginary line separating the reservation lands from Texas

or the Cherokee Outlet they no doubt soon came drifting
back again. Also, herds belonging to owners that claimed to
be taking them to various points in Kansas crossed the reservation in many places in spite of notices posted by the agent
warning all drovers to keep to the authorized trails. It is
certain that a number of men were occupying ranges on this
reservation during the summer and fall of 1882 and that they
were little disturbed though doubtless many of them had
some kind of private arrangement with the Indians.

One firm so occupying these lands with cattle was the
Standard Cattle Company, whose President was G. R.
Blanchard, Vice-President of the Erie Railroad. Among its
prominent stockholders were N. K. Fairbank, Samuel Johnston, Stephen F. Gale, William T. Baker, and Edson Keith.
This company occupied a range in the Cheyenne-Arapaho
country early in June, 1882, by making arrangements to pay
the Indians for the grass. Late in that year they grew afraid
that they might be disturbed and sent their general manager,
A. T. Babbett, to Washington to interview the Secretary of
the Interior. In this mission Babbett had the good offices of
no less person than Robert T. Lincoln, Secretary of War.
Lincoln wrote him a letter addressed to the Secretary of
the Interior requesting the latter to give Babbett his attention as he was the representative of some gentlemen in Chicago who were old friends of Lincoln's.

Apparently the fears of the Standard Cattle Company
were well founded for the fame of Indian Territory as a
grazing region was spreading and many people were eager
to secure ranges there. The pressure became so great at last
that Agent Miles evidently decided to proceed as he thought
best and then consult his superior officers about what had
already been done rather than court refusal by asking per-

mission to grant grazing privileges as he had done the previous summer. He accordingly sought, in December, 1882, to bring to a culmination plans he had made to lease a large part of the reservation under his jurisdiction to a group of cattlemen for a long term of years.

On December 12, 1882, the chiefs and warriors of the Cheyennes and Arapahoes met in council and filed a written request to be permitted to lease some 2,400,000 acres of their lands to ranchmen for grazing purposes at a price of not less than two cents an acre. One-half of the money should be used in buying young cattle for the Indians. The lessees were to be allowed to fence the land and might cut timber for that purpose from the reservation but all such fences were to become the property of the Indians when the lease had expired. This request was signed by sixteen Cheyenne and nine Arapaho chiefs.

This request, which was evidently put in form by Miles or some of the agency employees under his direction, was forwarded to the Commissioner of Indian Affairs, but without awaiting the action of that official a second council of chiefs and headmen met on January 8, 1883, and authorized Miles to make arrangements to lease all or any part of the lands mentioned in the request of December 12.

Leases were immediately signed by seven cattlemen who had evidently helped Miles in planning the entire transaction. These men were Edward Fenlon, of Leavenworth, Kansas; William E. Malaley, of Caldwell, Kansas; Hampton B. Denman, of Washington, D. C.; Jesse S. Morrison, of Darlington, Indian Territory; Lewis M. Briggs, of Muscotah, Kansas; and Albert G. Evans and Robert D. Hunter, of St. Louis. The leases aggregated a little more than three million acres and the documents granting them were all exactly alike.

Fenlon, Malaley, and Denman each were to have about 570,-
000 acres; Hunter, 500,000; Evans, about 457,000; Briggs,
318,000; and Morrison, a little less than 140,000. The term
of the leases was ten years, the rate two cents an acre payable
semiannually in advance, and the Indians might take all or
any part of any payment in cattle. In such case the value
of the cattle was to be determined by two commissioners,
one appointed by the Indian agent and one by the ranchman
making the payment or in case of a disagreement these two
might appoint a third. The provisions in regard to fencing
were included and it was made the duty of the Indians and
the Indian Bureau to see that the lessee had exclusive use
of the land during the term of his lease.

The lessees took copies of all these leases and placed them
in the hands of one of their number who was instructed by
Miles to proceed to Washington and secure the approval of
the Secretary of the Interior. The documents, however,
were never presented to the Indian Bureau, probably because
the ranchmen felt it was better to await a more favorable
time. There was some indication that the Commissioner of
Indian Affairs was considering modifying his attitude toward
grazing on the lands of the Indian Territory as in January,
1883, he sent to the Secretary of the Interior eight or nine
letters of inquiry with respect to grazing privileges in that
region and asked for instructions with the statement that he
would take no action with regard to these or any other appli-
cations that might be received until the pleasure of the Secretary was made known.

In the meantime the action of Agent Miles had brought
forth a storm of protest from certain cattlemen pasturing
herds on his reservation who had not been included in the
group making the so-called leases. B. H. Campbell, who

had been pasturing a large number of cattle on the reservation for some time, had written Miles just before the first Indian council had been held offering $50,000 for a lease for fifteen years of all that portion of the Cheyenne-Arapaho reservation lying west of a line drawn north and south approximately eighteen miles west of the agency. Campbell said that if the area mentioned was regarded as too large he would take a smaller area at a proportional figure. He asked that a council of the Indians be called to consider his proposition and that the matter be referred to Washington with such endorsements as would insure a speedy answer. Miles forwarded this letter to the Commissioner of Indian Affairs but stated later that the tract in question included some land that the Indians wished to reserve for themselves and made the recommendation that when leases were made about four tracts should be leased in order to give abundant grass and water to each lessee. When Miles made the leases about a month after the receipt of Campbell's letter leaving the latter entirely out, Campbell was naturally indignant and sought the aid of powerful friends in presenting his case to the Department of the Interior. An explanation was sought of the agent but Miles defended himself by saying that Campbell wanted some land which the Indians wished to retain for their own use and that he had asked for a fifteen-year lease while the other men had been content with ten. He said that so far as Campbell's claim to priority was concerned other applications had been on file for years and many men were insisting that they should have been considered. He disclaimed any intention of dealing unfairly with Campbell but said that the Indians had a right to lease to whom they pleased and that they would stand by the agreement made. He sent the Commissioner a list of the lessees and spoke in glowing terms of the benefits that must accrue to the Indians from the arrangement made. It is clear that Campbell had an excellent claim for consideration but it was not heeded though he fought hard and protested bitterly against what he plainly intimated was a corrupt bargain between Agent Miles and a "ring of cattlemen."

No evidence can be found, however, that Miles was corrupt or that he was not entirely conscientious in what he did, though it is quite evident that he and the group of cattlemen who secured the leases planned the entire enterprise together and that he favored them to the exclusion of others. This is apparent when we study the background and early history of the men who received the leases. Malaley was a former employee of the agency and apparently somewhat of a protégé of Miles. The latter had formerly sent him with parties of Indians going westward to the plains to hunt buffalo to watch over the hunting party and see that it did not turn its attention to raiding and horse-stealing in Texas. Morrison had lived on the reservation for some years, where he had married an Indian woman who bore him two children. She had died before 1882, however, and the children were in an Indian school. Briggs was a resident of Muscotah, Kansas, the town in which Miles had formerly lived when he was agent for the Kickapoo tribe which was located near by. Hunter and Evans had been partners for some time. They were formerly beef contractors who supplied beef to these Indians and other tribes in the western part of Indian Territory so were, of course, well known to Miles. Fenlon had also been a beef contractor and freighter and the agent had known him for years. The last of the lessees, Denman, was a resident of Washington, D. C., and it may be assumed that he was thought to have influence in the capital city and so might be able to prevent interference by the Department of the Interior.

The action of Agent Miles brought the matter of grazing upon the lands of the Indian Territory to an issue and resulted in the formation of a policy by the Department of the Interior with respect to the whole question of pasturing cattle upon Indian reservations. The intruding cattlemen who had not been included among the lessees did not remove their herds, so early in April, 1883, Edward Fenlon made a trip to Washington to take the matter up with the Secretary of the Interior. To this official Fenlon stated that part of the land leased was still occupied by the cattle of men who had ranches in Texas or elsewhere and he asked that the agent be directed to remove these men and put him in possession of his lease. He also asked instructions about when and how the money should be paid to the Indians.

To this the Secretary replied in a letter which laid down the future policy of the Department with respect to grazing upon Indian lands. He stated that it was not the policy of the Department to recognize affirmatively any leases or agreements of the character mentioned, but that he saw no objection to allowing the Indians to grant permission to parties desiring to graze cattle upon their lands on fair and reasonable terms subject to such supervision as the Department might think was necessary in order to prevent the Indians' being imposed upon. Such permission, he said, must be granted by proper authority and the benefits participated in by the whole tribe and not merely a favored few. Indian herders should be employed as far as possible. The Department would see to it that no permanent improvements were erected and no disreputable persons permitted to enter the reservation. The ranchmen and their employees must conform strictly to the law and the rules of the Department with regard to the introduction of firearms and ammunition or liquor. Payment should be made so far as possible in cattle. The letter closed with the following statement of policy:

"While the Department will not recognize the agreement or lease you mention, nor any other of like character, to the extent of approving the same, nor to the extent of assuming to settle controversies that may arise between the different parties holding such agreements, yet the Department will endeavor to see that parties having no agreement are not allowed to interfere with those who have. Whenever there shall appear just cause for dissatisfaction on the part of the Indians, or when it shall appear that improper persons, under the cover of such lease or agreement are allowed in the Territory, by the parties holding such agreements, or for any reason the Department shall consider it desirable for the public interest to do so, it will exercise its right of supervision to the extent of removing all occupants from the Territory without reference to such lease or agreement, on such notice as shall be right and proper under the circumstances under which the parties have entered the said Territory and have complied with the terms of the agreement and the instructions of the Department. All parties accepting such agreements should accept the same subject to all conditions herein and subject to any future action of Congress and this department as herein stated in relation to occupants of such Territory. Instructions will be issued to the agents in accordance with this letter."

The Department of the Interior had at last formulated a policy but such a policy as it was! It left the cattlemen without any assurance of tenure or protection whatever except that the Department would "endeavor to see to it that parties having no agreement are not allowed to interfere with those who have." On such uncertain tenure the Cheyenne-Arapaho lessees were expected to pay more than sixty thousand dollars a year for grazing privileges and to invest hundreds of thousands of dollars in cattle for the stocking of their ranges.

Such a system could hardly fail to provoke trouble. It placed a premium upon graft and corruption. Instead of putting the matter of grazing in the hands of some competent central authority, each case was left to the Indians of the reservation concerned who were nearly always more or less divided in opinion. This meant that it was often left to the agent but even so his hands were often tied and his actions embarrassed by factions and differences of opinion within the tribe. Cattlemen would be certain to offer to pay handsomely for favors and would come among the Indians and endeavor by gifts and flattery to secure their friendship and good will. A system was inaugurated analogous to the securing of "spheres of influence" by European nations among the tribes of Africa. Moreover, it was certain that men without agreements would be slow to remove and the Department of the Interior would meet with embarrassment in asking the military to remove them since these agreements had not been recognized. Such a system placed rival ranchmen in the position where they must intrigue to secure the favor of savage tribesmen and plot and scheme to get the ear of the agent and other governmental employees who might be expected to have influence with the Indians. It forced every man who sought to occupy Indian lands to resort to diplomacy and made every chief, half blood, or worthless squaw man a person to be courted, flattered, and, if possible, bribed in order to secure his favor.

In defense of the Secretary of the Interior it must be stated that he evidently considered that he had no authority in law to approve such leases or agreements. No opinion had been handed down to that effect at this time but such opinion was given about two years later by Attorney General Garland, to whom the matter was referred by the Department of the Interior. The Secretary was merely seeking to do by extralegal means what he felt he could not do legally though it is difficult to understand why he did not realize the endless trouble that was certain to follow the adoption of any policy so absurd as this.

Copies of the Fenlon letter were sent to the various agents for their guidance in the matter of grazing and the seeds of discord and strife thus planted quickly grew and bore fruit. The lessees on the Cheyenne-Arapaho reservation paid, on July 1, their first semiannual installment of lease money. The amount was more than $30,000 and as the Indians demanded silver Fenlon acted as paymaster and brought four pack-horse loads of silver dollars to the agency to make the payment. Arrangements were made for fencing and stocking their ranges but troubles came thick and fast. "Barbecue Campbell," after a hard fight, apparently despaired of success and removed his cattle temporarily to the Oklahoma Lands, after receiving assurances from the Secretary of the Interior that he would not be disturbed so long as he did not attempt a permanent occupation of that region.

There were a number of other men on the reservation, however, and some of them began to make trouble. Prominent among these were Dickey Brothers, previously mentioned, who had a large range in the northern part of the reservation and the southern part of the Cherokee Outlet on which they were holding a herd of 22,500 head. They had occupied this range about three years before under an arrangement made with a small band of Indians living in that vicinity to whom they made irregular payments in the form of beef and money. As a result these Indians were quite friendly and did not wish to see the Dickeys remove since the latter paid them more in beef and money than their share of the lease money would be. Two or three half bloods and squaw men associated with this band made the difficulty infinitely worse from the standpoint of Agent Miles and the lessees. This band of Indians refused to take their share of the lease money and, no doubt encouraged by Dickey Brothers and other trespassing cowmen, began to cause trouble.

In July an official of the agency accompanied by forty Indian police visited the ranch of Dickey Brothers and demanded that they remove, threatening serious consequences if they failed to comply with the order. They promptly refused and appealed to the Commissioner of Indian Affairs stating that their herds could not be removed at this time without entailing heavy loss and that they would submit to any terms if only they might be permitted to remain for a time at least.

The Commissioner at once notified Agent Miles that he interpreted that part of the Secretary's letter referring to "parties having no agreements with the Indians" as meaning trespassers pure and simple who placed cattle upon Indian lands without consent and who paid no compensation whatever whereas Dickey Brothers had an arrangement with some of the Indians, paid valuable consideration, and had apparently been allowed by Miles to remain for three years and to greatly increase their herds. It would therefore be unjust to require them to remove at once since they plainly had rights that could not be safely ignored. Miles was therefore ordered to allow them to remain for the present or until a careful investigation could be made and the results reported to the Department of the Interior and its decision rendered.

Such an interpretation of the Secretary's letter made the situation even more impossible than before, since it apparently meant that agreements did not have to be approved by the agent in charge of the reservation concerned. Under such an interpretation any ranchman might give a few Indians a little money or some beeves and claim to have paid valuable consideration and to have secured the consent of a part of the tribe to his occupation of Indians lands with cattle.

One paragraph of Dickey Brothers' letter to the Commissioner is significant. After asking that the lessees of the Cheyenne-Arapaho lands be prohibited from causing them the loss of their herd or great sacrifice by being obliged to sell it at that time they stated that "unless aided by the Department they cannot injure us and we therefore make this appeal." Evidently Dickey Brothers felt quite competent to take care of themselves unless interfered with by the United States government. In such fashion did range wars between rival cattlemen often begin.

When these men received from the Commissioner notice of the instructions sent to Agent Miles they evidently felt that they had won the first round of their battle and were thus encouraged to keep up the struggle. Aided no doubt by other cattlemen who had not been included in the leases made, they continued to intrigue with their Indian friends with the result that a party of these led by two or three squaw men left the reservation and hastened to Fort Supply in the Cherokee Outlet. To the commanding officer of that post, Colonel J. H. Potter, they complained bitterly of Agent Miles and said they had not signed the lease and had not wished to lease their land for a long term of years but that the agent had told them they must do so or he would refuse to issue their rations. They concluded by asking permission to go to Washington to present their grievances to the Secretary of the Interior.

Potter reported the presence of these Indians at Fort Supply to General Pope, who at once transmitted the report to the Secretary of War with the request that the matter be laid before the proper authorities as it was plain that some misunderstanding existed which might at any moment result in serious trouble.

Miles, upon learning that these Indians had left the reservation, telegraphed the commanding officer at Fort Supply to order them to return and to arrest them and any men with them in case they refused. He also wrote to the Commissioner of Indian Affairs explaining the difficulty, declaring that the Indians had no reason to complain, and asking that if they reached Washington they be returned to the reservation at once. Later, he wrote other letters replying to the request of the Commissioner for a complete report. In these letters he declared that the whole trouble was due to the fact that Dickey Brothers and other trespassing cattlemen had tampered with the Indians and that if more serious trouble occurred it would be due entirely to their work. He admitted that this band of Indians had refused to take their share of the lease money but said they had been present at the council when it was unanimously decided to lease the lands and had made no objection. The difficulty arose when some cattlemen had later told them that the lease was in reality a sale of their lands. He denied that rations had been withheld from these Indians and protested bitterly against Dickey Brothers' being permitted to remain on the reservation since he asserted that they could remove their herd without suffering great loss and that the money they claimed to have paid the Indians had nearly all gone to Wells and Chapman and in any case was no great amount. Fortunately, the Indians agreed to return to the reservation when ordered to do so by Colonel Potter but they remained sullen and discontented while Dickey Brothers and other ranchmen without leases no doubt stirred them up and kept them ready for further mischief.

While these difficulties on the northern part of the reservation were still unsettled, fresh trouble broke out in the southern and eastern part. The boundary line between the Cheyenne-Arapaho and the Kiowa-Comanche and Wichita reservations was in dispute, and when the lessees began to fence their land as a matter of convenience to aid them in caring for their cattle as well as for protection against trespass, the Kiowas and Wichitas commenced to protest and claimed that the ranchmen were fencing lands that belonged to them. Inspector Townsend, of the Indian Bureau, visited this region and made a report on the boundaries but the Wichitas were influenced by an attorney in New York by the name of Luther H. Pike, who visited these Indians, since he claimed to be attorney for them, and aroused them by stating that Townsend was dishonest and that he had made a dishonest report.

Early in November a delegation of Wichitas and Caddoes came to Agent Hunt at Anadarko and in a most insolent manner declared that the fencing of these lands must be stopped and that if Hunt refused to stop it they would do it themselves. Hunt at once notified Miles that these Indians meant mischief and that Miles had best be prepared to meet it if he could.

Hunt and Miles accordingly directed a joint letter to the Commissioner of Indian Affairs asking that the boundary between the reservations be resurveyed as nothing else would satisfy the Indians. Funds for this work were not available, however, and though the ranchmen offered to pay for having it done, the Secretary refused to accept their offer on the ground that the matter was too important to permit of its being paid for by private parties.

The lessees had formed themselves into an association called the Cheyenne-Arapaho Live Stock Association and in the spring of 1884 made an earnest appeal to the Commissioner to survey the boundary as they said that Indians were daily passing north of what they believed was the line and driving off or killing their cattle as well as animals belonging to the Cheyennes and Arapahoes. They said that the Kiowas were committing these depredations under the pretense that they were still on their own land and that these cattle were trespassing. They said that they would gladly meet the entire cost of the survey for until the line was definitely determined they felt sure there would always be trouble. This letter was referred to the Secretary of the Interior but that official replied that he was "not prepared to allow this survey to be done by the parties named, nor under their direction nor at their expense."

From the point of view of the cowmen it was very unfortunate that the active and resourceful Miles resigned on April 1, 1884, and was replaced by D. B. Dyer, former agent of the Quapaw reservation.

Whatever may have been the truth of the allegations as to Miles's relations with "a ring of cattlemen," he was a man of rare ability and tact in dealing with Indians. For ten years and more he had held the position of agent of these wild

tribes and had governed them with consummate skill. He
had seen war on his reservation and the ringleaders arrested
and taken away in irons. He had taken charge of these Indians when they subsisted mainly by hunting prairie buffalo,
had seen the disappearance of these animals, and issued tens
of millions of pounds of beef to his charges. Through it all
he had shown rare courage and ability.

The man who came to succeed him was a different type.
Clearly he had neither the resourcefulness nor tact of his
predecessor. His previous experience had not fitted him for
the difficult task he must now assume. Much pleased at first
over this appointment which he seemed to regard as a great
promotion, his joy was soon changed to grief and misgivings.
Unequal as Dyer was to the task confronting him it must be
admitted, in justice to him, that it is doubtful that any man
could have stayed the coming storm and brought order out
of the chaos that had developed on the reservation, mainly
as a result of the ineptitude and shortsighted policy of the
Department of the Interior.

The last official act of Agent Miles before his resignation
had been to ask for troops to eject the Kiowas from the
Cheyenne-Arapaho reservation and to restrain their depredations, which were of course mainly directed against the
cattle of the lessees. His request had been made to Major
Thomas B. Dewees, the commanding officer at Fort Reno.
That officer forwarded this request to Brigadier General
C. C. Augur, who had succeeded Pope as commander of
the Department of the Missouri, and that officer forwarded
it to his division commander with the statement that since
the Department of the Interior had refused to commit itself
to these leases by recognizing or approving them he had
ordered Major Dewees not to send troops until the views

of the War Department could be ascertained in the matter.

This communication was forwarded to the Secretary of War and was by him transmitted to the Department of the Interior. The Secretary of the Interior replied that the difficulty doubtless arose because of a difference of opinion with respect to the boundary and said that he thought there was no occasion for military interference. He stated further that it was "not the intention of the Department to attempt to protect the parties having permits for grazing privileges from the Indians, in their possession, except in so far as may become necessary to protect the Indians in the right to grant such permission as is given them by the provisions of section 2117 of the Revised Statutes."

This statement of the Secretary of the Interior was most significant. If it meant anything at all, it meant that men having permission to graze cattle on Indian lands had no protection from the Indians whatever, except what might be afforded them by the agent or in so far as they might be able to protect themselves. It was a virtual loosing of the Indians to prey upon the lessees' herds without let or hindrance so far as the Department of the Interior was concerned.

Naturally disorder grew and depredations increased. Agent Dyer in a panic sent call after call for troops. No less than six such requests were made by him between May 1 and the latter part of August, but all of these, incredible as it may seem, were entirely disregarded.

The Cheyennes and Arapahoes, no doubt encouraged by the failure to restrain the Kiowas, grew daily more insolent and troublesome and their depredations also steadily increased. Early in May war seemed actually at hand when one of the Cheyenne chiefs, Running Buffalo, attempted to levy toll on a herd of horses that a white man named Horton was conveying along the trail across the reservation and was shot and killed by the white man. In this case troops were actually sent out from Fort Reno to protect Horton, but the Indians seized half the horses as indemnity and the drovers in charge of the remainder were protected by Indian police until they were off the reservation with the remainder of their herd.

This was but one example of numerous acts of lawlessness. Dyer reported that certain bands of Indians stopped all persons crossing the reservation and demanded tribute. A white herder who came upon an Indian skinning a stolen beef was murdered. Some of the Indians lived ninety miles away from the agency and the agent could exercise but little supervision over them. Dyer reported that they wished to establish their camps at remote places where they could more easily depredate upon cattle without interference from the agency.

Agent Dyer's first annual report made under the date of August 9, 1884, was extravagantly pessimistic. He reported his Indians as numbering 6,271 though a later count showed the number to be less than four thousand. Dyer said that it was impossible to control them, that the cattlemen must have lost $100,000 the past year by depredations, and that this loss added to the grass payment made the cattle business on the reservation anything but profitable. He said that the loss the preceding winter from starvation had also been heavy and that skeletons dotted the prairie everywhere about the agency.

In the late summer of 1884 Inspector Robert S. Gardiner was sent to the Indian Territory to investigate conditions. He reported that Agent Dyer was quite right in his recommendations since there were more than six thousand Indians on the reservation and only 268 soldiers at Fort Reno, which was a force entirely inadequate to restrain the Indians, should the latter actually go to war. By this time additional leases had been made so that there were now nearly four million acres under lease at an annual rental of more than $76,000.

Early in December, 1884, Agent Dyer went to Washington to present in person his request to the Commissioner of Indian Affairs for aid. He reported that conditions were now worse than ever before and that the daily threats and constant depredations upon government cattle, as well as those of lessees, trail drivers, and beef contractors, could be checked only by a strong military force.

Apparently his arguments were convincing for the Secretary of the Interior now called upon the War Department for a strong force to be sent to the Cheyenne-Arapaho reservation to restore order. In the meantime, however, the ranching business in the Indian Territory had attracted the attention of many members of Congress and when that body met in December, Senator Vest, of Missouri, had presented a resolution asking for a Senate investigation of leases in the Indian Territory.

The result was a long and tedious Congressional investigation. This was just beginning when Secretary Teller made his request for troops. Also it was midwinter and thus difficult for troops to be placed in the field. All this tended to delay action. No force was sent and in the meantime the change of administration on March 4, 1885, further helped to delay definite action. In the meantime the situation on the Cheyenne-Arapaho reservation grew still worse and by June was so bad that the new Commissioner of Indian Affairs, Adkins, requested the Secretary of the Interior to ask the

War Department to put enough troops on the reservation to preserve peace. He also asked that the Indians be disarmed, Agent Dyer relieved and a new agent put in his place, and that all leases be declared annulled and the ranchmen and their herds removed from the reservation.

The Secretary promptly made the request and the War Department concentrated all troops in the West available for this purpose and sent them to the Cheyenne-Arapaho reservation. On July 10, the President himself asked Lieutenant General Sheridan to go to the agency and take charge of the situation. Upon his arrival at Fort Reno with a strong force, Sheridan reported that a part of the Cheyenne tribe numbering about twelve hundred was much disaffected in regard to the leasing of their lands for grazing. Yet, he said that all employees of the agency favored these leases, that all the proceedings in regard to them had taken place at the agency and that the name of Agent Miles appeared in all of them in his official capacity as agent. He stated that there were about 210,000 head of cattle on the reservation and that each of the leases had been fenced. He declared that the ranchmen had complied with their agreement and paid the lease money promptly and regularly and that the Indians had caused much loss and annoyance by killing the lessees' cattle at any time rations happened to be short. He said, however, that through no fault of the lessees their camps and ranches had become the headquarters of a roving, restless set of adventurers, whose influence upon the Indians was bad. He closed his report with the statement that the agent had lost the confidence of the Indians and recommended that he be removed and the reservation placed in charge of an army officer.

Even before the receipt of Sheridan's report, President

Cleveland had issued a proclamation in which he declared all leases on the Cheyenne-Arapaho reservation void, that the persons on these lands were there unlawfully, and that they must remove within forty days taking all cattle, horses, and other property with them. At the same time the President ordered Captain Jesse M. Lee to proceed to the reservation to relieve Agent Dyer.

Captain Lee reached the agency late in July. He reported that the cattlemen removed in good faith but that only one or two of them were able to get out within the time specified. Though the removal was accomplished with little friction, Lee asserted that the ranchmen had suffered heavy losses as a result but that he thought it a good thing to stop leasing and compel the Indians to go to work.

With the removal of all cattle from the Cheyenne-Arapaho reservation the ranching industry there came to an abrupt termination for a time at least. The cattlemen later asserted that Cleveland by his action compelling immediate removal from the Cheyenne-Arapaho reservation struck the ranch cattle interests of the United States a blow from which they never recovered. This seems a broad statement and yet it doubtless contains at least an element of truth. Not only were the 210,000 head removed from the Cheyenne-Arapaho lands but it seems probable that the agitation and presence of soldiers caused the removal of many other cattle from the western part of the Indian Territory. It was too late in the season to attempt to drive these cattle to northern ranges and when thrown upon the already overstocked pasture lands near by in Texas, the Cherokee Outlet, or Southern Kansas, they still further depleted those ranges and so were doubtless a great factor in causing the frightful losses in this region during the winter of 1885–86.

At any rate the summer of 1885 seems to have marked a turning point in the history of the ranch cattle industry. Two weeks after the proclamation ordering all cattlemen to remove from the Cheyenne-Arapaho reservation, President Cleveland issued a second proclamation ordering the removal of all wire fences from lands of the public domain and calling upon United States officials everywhere to aid in the execution of this order. This order, coupled with the enforced removal of the herds from the Cheyenne-Arapaho lands, was a crushing blow to the ranching interests. From this time on the ranch cattle industry declined as rapidly as it had formerly risen, constantly assailed by hostile public opinion, depressed by a steady decline in prices, and above all by the terrible losses of the winter of 1886–87, which left almost every cattleman on the northern plains bankrupt. The removal of the cattlemen from the Cheyenne-Arapaho reservation seems to have marked the beginning of that decline. It was the first step in the downward trend of an industry whose spectacular rise forms the theme of one of the most remarkable chapters in the economic history of the United States.

Sorry as was the state of affairs that had developed upon the Cheyenne-Arapaho reservation and which required for its final adjustment the strong arm of the military the blame for it rested not upon the cattlemen but upon the departments of government that failed to adopt some definite policy for dealing with grazing upon Indian lands. The ranchmen, unable to obtain ranges in the Indian Territory by legal means, were forced to secure indirectly and by ways that were devious and mysterious what they would gladly have secured at a fair price by open negotiation. It was ever so with the men who pastured herds along the far-flung frontier of American civilization. When they sought aid and protection from their government they met in many cases only suspicion and in some cases open hostility. No industry has been more maligned, misunderstood, and vilified than has the range cattle industry. Fortunately, history has at last begun to do justice to the brave men who risked their lives and fortunes on the broad plains of the Cow Country and to recognize that they were in truth "heralds of empire" and advance agents of civilization who builded better than they, or anyone else, could at that time know.

IX

The Cherokee Strip Live Stock Association

*Where are the men who in eighty-three
Rode the Cherokee Strip with me?
Parson, Shorty, Red, and Slim,
Ranicky Bill and Mexico Jim;
Nearly all of that gallant band
Have gone up the trail to the Glory Land.
And I must admit what I'm often told
That I myself am growing old.
So it can't be long 'till again I see
Those old Strip riders of eighty-three.*

RIDERS OF THE CHEROKEE STRIP

A<small>T THE BEGINNING OF THE NINETEENTH</small> century the Cherokee Nation of Indians occupied a large territory in northern Georgia. That state was eager to be rid of them and of the Creeks living farther south and accordingly made an agreement with the government of the United States in 1802 by which Georgia agreed to cede her western lands to the United States on condition that the latter remove the Indians from Georgia as soon as it could be done peacefully and on favorable terms. The following year came the purchase of Louisiana, affording a great region into which the Indian tribes might be removed, and in 1817 came the first Cherokee removal treaty. By this about one-third of the Cherokees gave up their lands in Georgia, receiving in exchange an equal area in western Arkansas to which they at once removed. The Cherokee Nation thus became divided into two parts—a western group in Arkansas known as the Cherokees West, and a larger eastern group in Georgia called the Cherokees East.

The western Cherokees soon became dissatisfied with their location owing to the fact that a few whites had settled on their grant of lands and refused to leave. Accordingly, in 1828 a treaty was made with the United States by which these Cherokees West gave up their lands in Arkansas in exchange for a grant of seven million acres in northeastern Oklahoma and a perpetual outlet nearly one degree in width extending west from their lands as far as the western boundary of the United States, at this time the one-hundredth meridian. This was the origin in the Cherokee Outlet, usually known in the history of Oklahoma as the "Cherokee Strip." Ten years after the western Cherokees had received this cession and removed to Oklahoma, their brethren in the East gave up their lands in Georgia and came west to join them and the nation was again united.

There was abundant room for all in the Cherokee country proper, so the Outlet remained entirely unoccupied and almost untouched by the Cherokee people. Hunting parties sometimes traversed it on their way to or from the buffalo ranges farther west, but that was all. No Cherokees made their homes there nor did they use it to pasture herds of cattle or other livestock.

In 1861 the Cherokees, in common with all the other nations of the Five Civilized Tribes, made an alliance with the Southern Confederacy. This alliance a portion of the Cherokees later renounced with the result that the war ended with the tribe divided into two bitterly hostile factions. By the treaty of Washington in 1866, the Indians of Oklahoma were compelled to give up a large part of their western lands to furnish homes for other tribes of the plains. However, the Cherokees received somewhat more liberal terms than did other tribes. They were not forced to give up any of their lands in Oklahoma but were required to allow the United States to locate friendly tribes upon the lands of the Outlet, though the title to the Outlet remained with the Cherokees until such tribes were so located. These new tribes brought in were to purchase the lands at a price agreed upon between them and the Cherokees, and, in case they could not agree, the United States had the right to fix what the price would be.

Under the terms of this treaty the United States during the next few years removed to this region the Osages, Kaws, Poncas, Otoes, and Missouris, and the Tonkawas. Each of these tribes purchased, or had purchased for them, a reservation in the eastern part of the Cherokee Outlet. The Pawnee reservation, composed largely of lands ceded by the Creeks, also extended across the line into the Outlet. All of those tribes were located in the eastern part of this territory, thus cutting off the unoccupied portion from the country of its owners, the Cherokees.

That unoccupied portion still remaining to the Cherokees was large. It had a length of more than 150 miles, a width of nearly sixty miles, and contained more than six million acres. Its area then was greater than that of either Massachusetts, New Hampshire, Vermont, or New Jersey, or about equal to that of either Holland or Belgium. To the north lay Kansas, to the west the long strip known as "No Man's Land" and the Panhandle of Texas, to the south the great Cheyenne-Arapaho reservation and the unoccupied area called "Old Oklahoma," and to the east the reservations of Osages and other Indians, and on beyond the country of the Cherokees.

The greater part of the Cherokee Outlet was excellent pasture land. The eastern portion was a region of level plains that has since proved one of the best agricultural areas in Oklahoma. The western part included wide stretches of low hills cut here and there by fertile valleys. It was watered by the North Canadian, the Cimarron, and the Salt Fork of the Arkansas together with the numerous tributaries of these streams.

The legal status of the Outlet was peculiar. The Cherokees had received a patent to their lands and so held them in fee simple. Their title to the Outlet was the same, subject only to the right given the United States in 1866 to locate friendly Indians there. Yet they could not legally settle upon it, owing to this right held by the United States, nor could it well be used for grazing, since it was separated from the Cherokee country proper by the reservations of the Osage and other tribes previously mentioned. The Cherokee Outlet was thus valuable property that might eventually by sale or lease bring the Cherokees a large sum of money but for more than ten years after the close of the Civil War they derived from it no revenue or benefit of any kind.

But though the Cherokees were not able to make use of the Outlet themselves, it was inevitable that as the ranching industry spread over the western plains herds of cattle should eventually be brought into that region by the ranchmen.

Some account has already been given of the beginnings and growth of the ranch cattle industry on the Great Plains as a whole. It is enough to repeat that it began on a gigantic scale soon after the Civil War and had its inception in the great state of Texas. Fostered by the Spanish land system and later by the huge grants given by Texas as a republic and as a state, ranching flourished in Texas on a large scale even before the outbreak of the Civil War. Also, during the four years of that conflict Texas remained the least touched of any southern state by the struggle. The result was that when the war ended and the Texas soldier-cowmen returned to their homes, they found their ranges overflowing with fine, fat cattle for which there was little market.

Earlier chapters describe the so-called northern drive. For many years following the war a great and ever-increasing stream of cattle poured northward to the cow towns of Kansas, from which they were either shipped to the markets of Kansas City, St. Louis, and Chicago or driven farther and spread out over the great ranges of the northern plains. Abilene, Newton, Ellsworth, Wichita, Caldwell, and Dodge City became famous shipping points and markets. Omitting the troublous year of 1866, the number of cattle driven north from Texas each year from 1867 to 1871 steadily increased and in the last named year the drive is estimated at six hundred thousand head. Most of these cattle were driven over trails leading across Indian Territory through the Cherokee Outlet.

The pasturing of Indian lands was forbidden by the Department of the Interior, but it was impossible to prevent the drovers from lingering along the trails if they so desired. Men with herds would turn aside from the main trail and stop for days, weeks, or even months to allow their cattle to gain in flesh before resuming the drive.

One of the best parts of the Indian Territory in which to do this was the Cherokee Outlet, entirely unoccupied by any Indians and remote from the home country of its owners. Other men, holding their herds in Kansas south of the cow towns while awaiting a buyer, drove them back into this region, where the grass was better than near the shipping points. Still others came to southern Kansas and established ranches and these men frequently allowed their cattle to stray across the line into the Cherokee Outlet or in many cases drove them across, seeking better pasturage.

In consequence, ranchmen in southern Kansas were by the early seventies pasturing many head of cattle in part at least on the Cherokee Outlet, while many herds from Texas were held there temporarily.

To this temporary occupation the Cherokees opposed at first no objection and in fact paid no attention. But as the years went by it is but natural that the rightful owners of this land should at last seek to derive some revenue from it. The first attempts were little more than demands for tribute by certain individual Cherokees who came to the Outlet and took up ranges under a sort of assumed headright. These Cherokees would allow a ranchman to bring his herd and pasture the cattle on or about the lands so claimed, thus giving a show of legality to the occupation. Many more men brought in cattle without any right whatever and established themselves upon ranges the boundaries of which the various men determined among themselves under the common law of the range, or "cow custom."

Since there was no fencing, the cattle of these ranchmen could not be kept entirely separate. Also, they mingled with "drift cattle" from Kansas or with the trail herds of "pilgrim cattle" from Texas. Boundaries were not always clearly defined and difficulties arose in determining the rights of each man.

In consequence of all these things, a meeting was held at Caldwell, Kansas, in the spring of 1880 to arrange plans for the spring roundup and in addition to consider other matters relative to grazing, particularly upon the lands of the Cherokee Outlet. At this meeting a permanent organization was formed and a date set for a meeting the following year.

Naturally the organization was a very loose one. Its purpose was to fix the date, place, and plan of roundups, to provide some method for settling disputes, and to take measures for protection against fire, thieves, wolves, and other destructive agencies. Yet it evoked in this region a squatter type of government not unlike that of the mining camps of the Rocky Mountains or the land claims associations of the Mississippi Valley or many other frontier organizations. It was organized, however, not to protect life and liberty, but property. The individuals caring for this property were comparatively few in number and in most cases felt quite competent to protect their own personal rights and liberties. What really required protection were their herds of cattle, valuable property that was placed in a region without law or courts and which was, by its nature, peculiarly open to attack.

As grazing in the lands of the Outlet increased, the authorities of the Cherokee Nation at last determined that it should be made to yield some revenue to the national treasury and in the summer of 1879 sent out one of its citizens to collect a grazing tax from all men pasturing herds there.

The amount collected this first year was small, but the following year Major D. W. Lipe, treasurer of the Cherokee Nation, came out and collected nearly eight thousand dollars. The rate was forty cents a head for grown cattle and twenty-five cents a head for all those under two years old. A receipt was given in the form of a grazier's license, which stated that the holder was permitted to pasture a certain number of head for a specified time.

In spite of the fact that the Cherokee treasurer opened an office at Caldwell and used his best efforts in collecting this tax, he was never able to secure payment for anything like all of the cattle that grazed on the Outlet lands. Men ranching in southern Kansas sometimes drove their herds into the Cherokee Outlet to avoid the payment of property taxes on them in Kansas and then drove them back home to avoid paying the grazing tax to the Cherokees.

In the meantime the crude association formed in 1880 was growing stronger. As more men brought cattle to the Outlet and the competition for ranges grew keener, it was necessary to improve the organization in order to settle disputes and arbitrate differences. This was all the more important since they had little or no protection of law and the courts and all realized the uncertain nature of their tenure of these lands.

The Department of the Interior had stated that it could not approve any lease of these lands for grazing, although it admitted that the Cherokees had possession of them and that they sometimes gave permits for that purpose. Therefore, the ranchmen realized how essential it was that their differences be settled among themselves and not brought to the attention of the Secretary of the Interior or other Federal authorities at Washington.

Encouraged by the fact that the Cherokees had adopted a regular system of issuing grazing permits, many ranchmen now began to construct wire fences to enclose their ranges. These were designed to facilitate the work of keeping their cattle within bounds and also to keep out drift cattle from Kansas. The fences were erected with the full knowledge and consent of the Cherokee treasurer, who believed they would make it easier to collect the grazing tax. Many of these fences were erected under the names of individual Cherokees.

As the business increased, it was inevitable that sooner or later these matters should be brought to the attention of the Department of the Interior, and in the early winter of 1882 this happened. Early in the autumn the ranching firm of

Scott and Topliff paid their grazing tax on a range in the Cherokee Outlet. A few weeks later two Cherokee Indians appeared with the representative of an organization known as the Pennsylvania Oil Company and set to work to fence a tract of two hundred thousand acres, including the range of Scott and Topliff.

This was clearly a matter for arbitration and should not have been taken to Washington. But the oil company was a great corporation apparently new at ranching and perhaps largely using that business as a cloak to conceal its prospecting for oil in southern Kansas and the Indian Territory. Its representatives cared little for cow custom and knew little of the danger involved in refusing to arbitrate. They began fencing at once, and Scott and Topliff, in anger and desperation, appealed to the Department of the Interior.

Only the barest outline of what followed can be given in so brief a chapter as this. Secretary Teller referred the letter of Scott and Topliff to Commissioner of Indian Affairs Price. The latter promptly began an investigation and soon reported to the Secretary of the Interior that fencing and other improvements on a large scale were under construction in the Cherokee Outlet. He said that the Attorney General had held that the Cherokee Nation had no right to settle its citizens in the Outlet, and yet many tracts were fenced there under the names of individual Cherokees, who had received large sums of money for the use of their names. He declared that this unauthorized settlement and improvement must be stopped and asked that the War Department be asked to furnish troops to remove or destroy all the improvements. Price also wrote the Indian agent for the Five Civilized Tribes instructing him with reference to what had been done and ordering him to give the ranchmen notice that they would be allowed twenty days to remove all fences and other improvements from the Outlet, failing which they would be removed by the military. When the twenty-day limit had expired, he was instructed to call upon the proper officer for troops to execute the order.

The most charitable view that can be taken of the attitude of the Secretary and Commissioner is that they were entirely ignorant of every detail of the range cattle industry. To destroy not only all fencing but camps and corrals as well in a region larger than the state of Massachusetts in which were grazing a quarter of a million head of cattle, and that, too, in midwinter, would be an act entirely indefensible, no matter under what circumstances these improvements had been erected.

Fortunately the War Department either had some realization of these things or else merely showed its usual reluctance to co-operate with the Department of the Interior. At any rate, the Secretary of War asked to be shown some provisions of law which would protect officers and soldiers in removing and destroying such improvements and the matter rested there for a time. Protests from the ranchmen came pouring into the Secretary of the Interior's office and Agent Tufts was at last instructed to hold his order to remove fences in suspension while he made a complete investigation, which should be reported to the Commissioner.

Tuft's report, made on March 1, 1883, was very favorable to the cattlemen. He found nearly one thousand miles of wire fencing on the Outlet. He recommended that this be allowed to remain and that more fencing be sanctioned, provided permission should be obtained from the Cherokees, and that all fences be subject to removal at once upon notice of the Department of the Interior.

The Secretary of the Interior now gave his decision that the ranchmen would be permitted to retain their improvements only after making satisfactory arrangements with the Cherokees.

While the Secretary and the Commissioner were trying to arrive at some decision with respect to ranching upon the Outlet, the ranchmen themselves had not been idle. Many of them were men of great ability with powerful political connections, and they were fully determined not to allow their large interests to be destroyed without making a desperate effort to save them. The plan now formulated was to transform the cattlemen's organization formed some years before into a real corporation and secure from the Cherokee government a long-time lease of the entire Outlet.

Unfortunately this latter step was rendered somewhat difficult by the political conditions in the Cherokee Nation. The tribe was at this time almost an independent republic with a principal chief, bicameral legislature, and system of courts. Political issues were closely drawn and the two chief parties, the Union and the National, were bitterly hostile toward each other.

The ranchmen now opened negotiations with the principal chief, Dennis W. Bushyhead, a man of education and real ability, who was favorable to them and their interests.

In March, 1883, Bushyhead visited Washington, where he had an interview with Secretary Teller and Commissioner Price. He promised them that upon his return he would call a special session of the Cherokee Council and consider the entire matter of grazing on the Outlet.

In the meantime the ranchmen held a meeting at Caldwell, Kansas, on March 6, 7, and 8. This was attended by virtually all cattlemen pasturing herds on the Outlet. A committee was appointed to draft a constitution and bylaws, and the new organization thus formed was incorporated under the laws of Kansas as "The Cherokee Strip Live Stock Association."

The purpose of the new corporation as stated in the charter was the "improvement of the breed of domestic animals by the importation, grazing, breeding, sale, barter, and exchange thereof." The term for which it was to exist was forty years, the number of directors nine, and the principal office and place of business was Caldwell, Kansas.

The bylaws were, like the constitution, very brief. They provided that all persons, corporations, or companies occupying an undisputed range in the Cherokee Strip and who agreed to pay the assessments might become members of the association upon payment of the membership fee of ten dollars. Each member had one vote and persons holding contiguous ranges outside the Outlet might be elected honorary members upon recommendation of the directors. This was apparently done in order that such persons might be given roundup privileges. All transfers of ranges by sale or otherwise were to be recorded in the books of the secretary, and all members must within thirty days after their admission to membership furnish the secretary with a description of the marks and brands of all domestic animals owned by them, which should be recorded by the secretary in a book kept for that purpose.

Curiously, neither constitution nor bylaws make any provision for such officers as president, secretary, and treasurer, though some of them are mentioned. However, a board of arbitration was created consisting of three members appointed by the directors. This board had power to settle all disputes, though an appeal might be taken to the board of directors by furnishing bond in a sum sufficient to pay all expenses of such appeal. Despite the fact that the constitution made no provision for officers, the directors met at once and chose Ben S. Miller as president, John A. Blair, secretary, and M. H. Bennett, treasurer.

It should be noted that this organization was peculiar. It was not a corporation in the ordinary sense of the term, since it had no capital stock and, in consequence, no stockholders. It was an association with a membership composed of individuals, partnerships, and corporations, many of the last named with a heavy capitalization and numerous stockholders. Operating in a region without law or courts, it had little authority for its acts except the general consent of its members and yet for seven years or more this great association, with no property except such as it obtained from assessments of its members, was one of the most powerful factors in the development of Indian Territory.

Upon Bushyhead's return to the Cherokee Nation he at once proceeded to carry out his promise to Secretary Teller and Commissioner Price and called the Cherokee National Council to meet in special session. The association, besides its regular attorneys, had employed John F. Lyons, of Fort Gibson, an intermarried citizen of the Cherokee Nation, as special attorney. He was a man of rare tact and ability who, of course, practiced influence rather than law. Lyons kept his employers informed of the situation in the Cherokee country and when the special session of the council met early in May, two directors of the association, Andrew Drumm and Charles Eldred, hastened to Tahlequah and remained there during the entire session of the council.

There was much difference of opinion in the council with respect to the matter of grazing, and also there were a number of other men there seeking a lease of the Outlet. However, the representatives of the association overcame all opposition and at last secured the passage of a bill giving to the Cherokee Strip Live Stock Association a lease of the entire Outlet for a term of five years in consideration of the sum of $100,000 a year, payable semiannually in advance. The bill was signed by the principal chief, May 19, and on the same day the two directors of the association filed with the chief their acceptance of the provisions of the act together with such terms and conditions as the chief might think necessary.

These provisions stated with considerable detail the terms under which the lease was made. The lessees bound themselves to erect no permanent improvements on the land, and such temporary improvements as might be necessary in caring for their cattle were to be the property of the Cherokee Nation upon the expiration of the lease. No timber was to be cut except for use in fencing or building necessary temporary structures. No person not a member of the association was to be permitted to graze stock upon the Outlet without the consent of the association. Finally, failure to make payment promptly was to work a forfeiture of the lease.

The actual lease was signed early in July. It was given to the nine directors in trust for the association. The matter was never presented to the Department of the Interior, though it is possible that Bushyhead may have talked it over informally with Secretary Teller, as he made a trip to Washington soon after the adjournment of the council, though he left no official report of what had been done with the Department.

The lease actually went into effect October 1, 1883, and

on that date the first payment of lease money was made. The Cherokees asked that it be made in silver and the treasurer of the association, Milton Bennett, took $50,000 in silver from Caldwell to Tahlequah, a long and dangerous journey to make at this time with so great a treasure.

The association now set to work to organize its affairs. The Outlet lands were surveyed and the boundaries of each range defined. Wide strips were left for trails across the Outlet and lands were also set aside for quarantine grounds, with the result that the total amount used for grazing was reduced to a little more than five million acres. This was divided among about one hundred individuals, corporations, and firms, but some four or five hundred men were included in the organizations while, including stockholders in the various companies, perhaps two thousand people were interested in the association.

Each member of the association was given a lease of his land by the directors for the entire period of five years. For this he was to pay one and one-fourth cents an acre every six months, though the first semiannual assessment was two cents an acre in order to give money enough to get the organization started. Each member then gave a series of promissory notes for the amount of the future payments, maturing on March 15 and September 15, or fifteen days before the semiannual lease payment must be made to the Cherokees. Each man erected his own fences, camps, and corrals. Tens of thousands more cattle were now brought in and the ranges heavily stocked. The board of arbitration decided all disputes. Hunters were employed to kill wolves, rewards were offered for the capture of thieves, and the improvement of breeds of cattle was encouraged. Within a year all difficulties had been settled and the association was not only a going concern but was running smoothly. It was the greatest livestock organization in the world and its power and influence were enormous. Troubles on the Cheyenne-Arapaho reservation to the south and rumors of bribery and corruption in securing the lease from the Cherokees resulted in a Congressional investigation of the ranchmen in Oklahoma in the winter of 1884–85. This investigation went the way of many other Congressional investigations. The charges of bribery and corruption could not be substantiated and the association was not seriously disturbed.

Soon after this investigation ended, the association decided to try to secure a renewal of their lease while their friend Bushyhead was still in office. The attempt was made at the regular session of the Cherokee Council in the autumn of 1886, but failed, and the only result was to set in motion further rumors of bribery and corruption.

At this session of the council there also appeared representatives of a syndicate that was seeking to purchase all the lands of the Outlet. The sum of three dollars an acre, or a total of eighteen million dollars, was offered, but of course the Cherokees could not sell without the consent of the United States.

At the winter session of the Cherokee Council in 1887–88, the association succeeded in securing the passage of a bill giving them a renewal of the lease for five years at $125,000 a year, but the principal chief, Joel B. Mayes, who had succeeded Bushyhead, vetoed the bill on the ground that others were offering more money.

A bitter fight was waged during the next year, ending at last in the approval of an act in the autumn of 1888 granting to the association a new lease for the period of five years in consideration of the sum of $200,000 a year.

It would seem that with the approval of this lease the association was in an excellent position. They had occupied this region for nearly ten years, the last five of which had been under a lease made with the full knowledge and apparent consent of the Department of the Interior, even though existing laws had prevented its formal approval.

But in spite of this promising outlook disasters were impending. The years of agitation for the settlement of the Oklahoma Lands just south of the Outlet had at last culminated in the opening of that region to settlement in April, 1889. Settlers came pouring across the Outlet to join in the race for homes in Oklahoma. Also the pioneer farmers, encouraged by the opening of the Oklahoma Lands, were clamoring to be allowed to settle still other areas, including the Cherokee Outlet. Railroads, border towns, wholesaling centers, and the press added their voices to the general tumult, all urging that these great areas in western Oklahoma occupied by few or no Indians should be settled by the whites. The opening of the Oklahoma Lands gave the pioneer settlers a foothold in the very center of the Indian country and made it inevitable that adjoining lands should also soon be opened to settlement.

Even before the settlement of the Oklahoma Lands, or in March, 1889, an act of Congress was approved creating a commission of three persons to negotiate with the Cherokees and other western tribes relative to the cession of their surplus lands. This act provided that the Cherokees should be offered $1.25 an acre for the Outlet and that, in the event of their acceptance, it should be opened to settlement. This body was known as the Cherokee Commission. It promptly set to work but soon found that the Cherokees were unwilling to sell at the price offered. This was natural, since a syndicate of cattlemen had already offered them $3.00 an acre for their lands, so they could hardly be expected to be willing to sell for less than half that sum.

The clamor for the opening of the Outlet lands to settlement steadily increased, but the Cherokee Commission could make no progress in its dealing with the Indians. This was due in part to the influence of the Cherokee Strip Live Stock Association, who were encouraging the Cherokees to refuse to sell. The matter was made more complicated by the question of title to the Outlet.

Secretary of the Interior Noble urged that the Cherokee title was very shadowy and that the United States had the right to take these lands if necessary, while the Commissioner of Indian Affairs, T. J. Morgan, asserted that the Cherokee title was perfectly good. Late in October Secretary Noble stated his policy in a letter to General Lucius Fairchild, chairman of the Cherokee Commission, who was then at Tahlequah. Noble stated that adverse and, it was believed, illegitimate influences had been brought to bear upon the Cherokees by the cattlemen. He reviewed the whole history of grazing upon Outlet lands and said that the leases of Indian lands for grazing were void and that the President had the authority to so declare them and to remove the ranchmen and their property by force. He declared that the offer of $1.25 an acre for the lands was under the circumstances munificent, while the title of the Cherokees even to use was precarious and likely to be defeated utterly. He criticized the "cattle syndicate" for its attempts to "rival and defeat the Government," and said it was acting in "defiance of law against public interest." He said that it was now deemed best to lay hands upon these pretended lessees and remove them and their property by force not later than

June 1, 1890. He said that if the United States found that its own title to the Outlet was good, it would not hesitate to take over these lands if the circumstances of the American people should require it. Noble closed by instructing Fairchild to make such use of the letter as he saw fit and to report whatever action he might take to the Department.

The letter from Noble was at once a warning and a threat. Public opinion demanded that the Cherokee Outlet be opened to white settlement. If the Cherokees refused to sell at the price fixed by the government of the United States, they should be punished. Their revenue from these lands was to be stopped, notwithstanding the fact that they had received such revenue regularly for ten years. At the same time a threat was made to take the lands by force if the United States found that it had the superior title. This would, of course, be determined by the United States itself and the Cherokees knew by bitter experience not to expect too much if the matter were pushed to an issue.

In the meantime the Cherokee Strip Live Stock Association was the victim. The Indians, so long as they received revenue from these lands, would not cede them for seven and one-half million dollars when private parties were offering them eighteen millions. In order to compel a cession, the ranchmen must be removed and all revenue cut off until such a time as the Cherokees were willing to yield.

Perhaps public interest demanded such a policy and yet it is difficult to defend. The ranchmen had been allowed to occupy these lands for ten years. A situation had not only been allowed to develop but had been encouraged and then a great productive industry was to be destroyed upon short notice. Worst of all, the men whose business was thus threatened had no recourse. No court could give them redress or protection, or even order that they be allowed time in which to arrange their affairs.

Recognizing the seriousness of the situation the association prepared and presented to the President a very able memorial setting forth their side of the case, but nothing could help the ranchmen very much at this time. The Department of the Interior, urged on by popular clamor, had determined to open the Cherokee Outlet to settlement. The most that the cattlemen could hope was that they might be given a reasonable time in which to adjust their affairs and market their herds.

Fortunately, President Harrison was more lenient than Secretary Noble. Having secured from the Attorney General an opinion that the lease of the association was without legal force, the President issued about the middle of February a proclamation forbidding all grazing on the lands of the Cherokee Outlet and ordering all cattle to be removed by October 1, 1890. When we consider that these lands were not opened to settlement until September, 1893, or almost three years later, it must be obvious that the purpose here was not to prepare the lands for settlement but that this was a political move directed against the Cherokees to force a cession of the lands.

For a time the Cherokees remained obdurate, but they, like the ranchmen, were fighting a losing battle. Early in 1891 a bill was introduced into Congress proposing to pay the Cherokees $1.25 an acre for the lands of the Outlet and take them without further negotiation. Noble favored this bill but the Commissioner of Indian Affairs disagreed entirely with his chief and said that for Congress to take these lands would be for the "Government to violate its faith and disregard its solemn obligations."

Fortunately the Cherokees were wise enough not to push the matter too far. When it became evident that they must either cede the lands or see them taken by an act of Congress, they decided to accept the inevitable and late in 1891 signed an agreement with the Cherokee Commission ceding the lands of the Outlet in consideration of the sum of a little more than eight and one-half million dollars, or about $1.40 an acre.

In the meantime the Cherokee Strip Live Stock Association had seen its last hope vanish with the issuance of the presidential proclamation. A brief extension of sixty days was secured, but December 1, 1890, was set as the final date for the removal of all cattle from the Outlet. Nothing remained for the ranchmen to do but to market such cattle as they could and remove the remainder to other ranges.

Chief Mayes, of the Cherokee Nation, brought suit against the association for the remainder of the lease money. The case was fought out in the courts of Kansas and at last won by the cattlemen, but this litigation with attendant costs and the constant appearance of debts and claims proved most discouraging. At last at a directors' meeting held in Kansas City in April, 1893, Vice-President Charles Eldred was given authority to sell or dispose of all notes, claims, and debts due the association. This he did soon after by transferring them to three members of the association who agreed in consideration of this transfer to assume all debts, notes, claims, and judgments against the organization. By this transaction the Cherokee Strip Live Stock Association ceased to exist and a few months later, in September, 1893, the region in which it had operated, the Cherokee Outlet, was opened to white settlement.

The Cherokee Strip Live Stock Association was for years

perhaps the greatest organization in the world engaged in the livestock industry and its influence upon the history of Oklahoma and Kansas was very great. Some significant features of its activities may be summed up as follows:

1. Here is to be seen an excellent example of the ability of the American pioneer to organize in a region without law or courts extralegal institutions that seemed to function with surprising efficiency and afford adequate protection to extensive economic interests.

2. The association in its relations with the Cherokees affords an example of the curious reactions secured when red men and white are brought together in business or political affairs. An illustration is also given of the rare political ability of the Cherokee people—an ability that has since that time put many persons of Cherokee blood into high official positions in Oklahoma.

3. In dealing with this association the Department of the Interior and most other officials of the United States showed a lack of understanding of the ranching industry, with the result that policies were adopted which were often unjust, inefficient, and in some cases little short of absurd.

4. Seeking as it did to discourage agricultural settlement of the Indian lands of Oklahoma, the association, by its very presence on these lands, did much to render such settlement inevitable.

5. The accusations made against this association by the pioneer farmers, the United States government, and the press served in time to develop a public opinion hostile to the ranching industry as a whole which, in certain sections of the country, has never entirely disappeared.

6. By its opposition to the opening of Indian lands to settlement, the association incurred the bitter hostility of the

agricultural population in Kansas and adjoining states. From this hostility toward wealthy cattlemen it was a natural step to hostility toward all forms of corporate wealth. The ranchmen were thus an important factor in the development of Populism in this region.

7. The opening of the Cherokee Outlet and other Indian lands in Oklahoma furnishes an example of the changing of the economic life of large areas by legislation. To say that the land was taken from the Indian and given over to white settlement is only nominally correct. The Indian as an economic factor was negligible. What really happened was that the land was taken from the ranchman and given to the farmer. Vast numbers of cattle were removed from these ranges and shipped to market and the ranges themselves almost immediately transformed into wheat fields. The result was important in the production of the cheap meat and bread of the early nineties.

8. Finally, the forced removal of the ranchmen from the Cherokee Outlet in order to deprive the Cherokees of further revenue and so force a sale of these lands at a price representing only a fraction of their value presents one of the latest and most glaring examples of injustice done the Indian by the government of the United States.

Part VI

The Passing of the Cow Country

X

The Cow Country in Transition

They came in covered wagons
And we didn't like them much—
These tenants from the Southland
With some Yankees, Swedes, and Dutch.
But they built their little dugouts
And turned over prairie sod,
Which was right side up already
By the handiwork of God.

COVERED WAGON PEOPLE

IVALRIES SERVE TO EXPLAIN many things in history. The rivalry between Athens and Sparta, Rome and Carthage, and England and Spain are all familiar Old World examples, while that between North and South, the industrial East and the agricultural West, and New York and Boston are equally familiar for the New. Similarly, rivalries have often existed not between cities, nations, or geographic regions, but between groups or certain social, economic, or racial orders within the same region. When the Anglo-American civilization struck the Spanish culture of the Southwest, when the English colonists came in contact with those of the French in Canada, or when the New England Puritans met and mingled with the German settlers of the Old Northwest, a struggle ensued over which racial element and which type of social order should prevail.

Out of this mingling of two societies came first conflict and eventually a fusion producing a new order unlike either of the first two, but with some of the attributes of both. So developed a regional society, growing from two stems, which continued for generations and which still bears fruit of a hybrid variety showing certain characteristics of both parent stocks.

If "it is a wise child that knows his own father," so is it a wise society which knows both its own father and its own mother, or the two dominant roots from which it sprang. Obviously, these are often more than two in number, but perhaps in most cases two are so much more important than the others that they may logically be called the parents of the existing society. The father of the present social order in most of that part of the western prairie states settled within the last two generations was the wild, roaring "cow country" of earlier days, while the mother might be said to be the agricultural society of the homesteaders coming from the wooded, or partially wooded, crop-growing region of small farmers farther east. The story of their introduction to one another and the ripening of their acquaintance until "these twain became one flesh" is a story which, so far as the writer knows, has never been told with any detail. Yet it is a most significant story which, if the figure of speech may be continued, proves conclusively the truth of Kipling's famous statement that "the female of the species is more deadly than the male." It indicates, too, that the bride did all the pursuing and, having won her mate by strong-arm methods, she eventually imposed upon him and upon the family most of her own ideas and ideals. The wild, roistering days of his youth were left behind. He and his children in time joined the wife's church, adopted her way of life, and settled down as sober, respectable citizens. Only occasionally does the offspring show an outcropping of that paternal wildness which had made its father a bit notorious in earlier years.

It is true that during the period of the honeymoon the groom made a more or less determined effort to induce his spouse to accept his guidance with regard to the conduct of their daily affairs of life, but in this he met with scant success. She was an obstinate and headstrong wench and he soon became impressed with the truth of the old rhyme:

> *A wedding is the greatest place*
> *For folks to go and learn*
> *He thought that she was his'n*
> *But he found that he was her'n.*

This union was to bear fruit in the years following the Civil War when a vast stream of cattle flowed north out of Texas and spread over the central and northern plains, while agricultural settlement hesitated for a time at the eastern edge of the great prairies. Even a half decade after Appomattox the states and territories forming the second tier west of the Mississippi were comparatively thinly peopled. At that time their unsettled area included nearly all of the Dakotas, the western three-fourths of Nebraska, two-thirds of Kansas, virtually all of Indian Territory except for the Five Civilized Tribes of Indians in its eastern one-third, and the western two-thirds of Texas. Much of this region was potentially valuable for the growing of crops and all of it, together with the broad expanse of more arid lands farther west, was wide open to occupation by cattle. Within two decades after the close of the war the range cattle industry had spread over virtually all of this vast territory and had reached the point of its greatest extent and the height of its importance.

So came into existence that vast pastoral empire commonly known as the Cow Country, in which society had for its economic basis cattle and the native pasturage upon which they fed. Like every pastoral society, it was mobile, with the people who composed it far less fixed in abode than were the crop-growing farmers farther east. True, some ranchmen owned in fee at least a part of the lands occupied by their herds and had built permanent homes where they lived with their families. Most of them, however, occupied temporary ranges upon the public domain or on Indian reservations where their tenure was most precarious. In such cases improvements were of flimsy and temporary construction, and the headquarters was merely the administrative center of their business. As conditions changed, these men would, in a few years, shift their operations and establish new headquarters or in some cases remove all or a portion of their cattle to new ranges quite remote from the original ranch. As for the cowboys who carried on the business, they seldom had any fixed abode which could properly be called a home. They occupied temporary line camps along the borders of a range. Here they might remain for only a few months, after which they would be transferred to some other camp. They followed the roundup wagon in the spring or autumn, accompanied herds of cattle on the long drive up the trail, left one outfit after a few months or a few years to seek employment with another, and were in general a wandering and restless group seldom occupying, for any considerable length of time, a fixed habitation.

The range area was peculiarly a man's country. One range rider has recorded that during a year's work he did not see a woman for nine months and the writer as late as 1904 visited a ranch in western Texas where the ranchman's wife asserted that she had not seen another woman for more than six weeks. Since women were so few in number, they were held in high esteem and treated with an almost exaggerated respect. Many a quick-witted cowboy known for his gay conversation and clever repartee with his own kind became a tongue-tied, stuttering moron when in the presence of a woman with whom he was but slightly acquainted. Yet some few of the ranchmen had wives and daughters who gave a feminine touch to their homes and who would occasionally arrange social affairs which people traveled long distances to attend. These were, in most cases, dances with few girls and many "stags" where the square dance, or quadrille, was the rule. Music was furnished by one or two fiddlers, assisted at times by some one to "beat the strings" with two heavy knitting needles or pieces of wire. If the home boasted a cottage organ and someone could be found to "second on the organ," so much the better. The dance often lasted all night with supper served at midnight. "We danced the last set after sunrise" was a proud boast meant to indicate a remarkably good time. Since girls were so few in number, some danced virtually every set—and after breakfast mounted their horses to ride fifteen to thirty miles to their homes.

Such dances furnished the average cow hand with almost his only opportunity for the society of women. His pleasures were few and simple. He sometimes had at his camp a few books or magazines and of course played cards if he had a partner or if some stray rider dropped in to spend the night. If on his rare visits to town he sought solace in a game of poker or a few drinks, he should be pitied for the loneliness of his life rather than blamed for his weakness or folly.

Into this rough, masculine society of the Cow Country eventually began to be projected a far different social order. Men from the settled regions to the east, eagerly seeking for "level land" upon which to establish homes, came in with their families in covered wagons, bringing not only strange tools and household goods, but even stranger ideas and ideals. Choosing 160-acre homesteads on the fertile plains, these men set to work to build homes, plow up the prairie sod, fence fields, and plant crops. Into a region of long-horned steers, hard-riding men, boots, spurs, branding irons, saddles, ropes, and six-shooters, they brought plows and hoes, pitchforks, churns, cook stoves, rocking chairs, feather beds, pillows, dogs, cats, pigs, and chickens, but most important of all, wives and children.

To a region of sour-dough bread, beef steak, bacon, dried apples, beans, flapjacks, and coffee were brought salt-rising bread, buttermilk biscuits, pies, cakes, doughnuts, preserves, jellies, custards, and fresh vegetables. To a vast area covered with cattle, these newcomers, curiously enough, brought milk and butter, articles of food from which the average cowpuncher shied as does a range horse from corn.

Most significant of all, these people brought the home, the school, the church, and the Sunday School to compete with the camp, saloon, dance hall, and gaming table. With all of these things they brought what was to the range country a new conception of life and of society—a new set of objectives to be attained.

The effects of the impact of this sober, settled, industrious farming population upon the more primitive pastoral society of the Cow Country were at once apparent. The range riders regarded these intruders with some contempt and suspicion, not unmixed with active hostility. They must inevitably be men of small ideas, since each was bound to a petty 160 acres of land, walked rather than rode, and worked at such menial tasks as plowing, milking cows, and feeding chickens. The ignorance and general wrongheadedness of many a newcomer were, moreover, alarming. He climbed on a horse like a man going up a ladder, could not read a brand, and if he owned a saddle at all, it was an antiquated structure, the very sight of which moved the punchers to spasms of laughter. His methods of doing business were mysterious and past finding out. The fence, designed to protect his field, consisted of one wire and a dog, and he possessed a "one way pocket book" wherein he hoarded diligently his few hard-earned dimes.

"I guess old man Johnson's maybe a nice old feller enough," said cow hand Bill Jones, "but he don't know nothin' at all about business. Why, he's savin' as hell."

"That's right," answered his companion. "You know th' other day he gave me a letter to mail and two copper cents to buy the stamp. I told him that nothin' less'n a nickel goes in this country."

"Just like him," replied Bill. "He may be all right in his way, but damn his way."

So spoke Bill Jones, and so spoke the Cow Country as a whole. The homesteader, commonly called the "nester," might be all right in his way, but it was a far different way from that of the range region, and the latter disapproved of it wholeheartedly. His penny-pinching tendency was but one of many unpleasant characteristics, but that alone was bad enough. Any man who had been known to refuse a respectable traveler a couple of meals and a night's lodging, or, even worse, to demand payment for such a trifling courtesy, was beneath contempt.

The range riders regarded themselves as far above any such petty meanness. In fact, until the coming of these homesteaders, such behavior was an unheard-of thing. A rider might stop at any cow camp certain of food and shelter and a cordial welcome. If the cowboy stationed at the camp happened to be absent, it did not matter. No lock was on the door, and any hungry traveler passing by was expected to go in and prepare himself a meal or spend the night if he wished, courtesy only requiring that he wash the dishes before leaving. The cow hands drew fair wages, had no families to support, and took very little thought of the morrow. Money, if they had it, was to spend. They bought drinks for the crowd, candy by the pound, wore expensive hats and gloves, and paid enough for one pair of boots to shoe the numerous issue of the homesteader for a whole year with something left over. If they wanted to shoot craps or play poker for high stakes when they were in town, who was to say them nay? It was their own money. If they lost it, they were sure of food and a place to sleep at any ranch or line camp in the whole great pastoral empire that was the Cow Country. Such minor courtesies as riding thirty miles to restore a strayed horse to the owner, lending a friend half a month's wages, or taking him a quarter of beef were a part of life. Would not anyone do the same? Of course he would, unless he happened to be one of these blue-nosed nesters!

The cow hands observed that their boss, who owned the ranch, carried on his business on the same basis, and they felt it must be the correct basis since he was a wealthy and successful man. His hospitality was boundless. Any stranger was welcome at the ranch and might stay as long as he liked. They had seen the ranch owner feed and care for from fifty to a hundred head of some neighboring ranchman's cattle all winter until the latter could come and get them. With many thousands of dollars in the bank he would give a common puncher a book full of checks signed in blank and start him out to buying steers, certain that every check would be filled out for exactly the correct amount required in each purchase. They had, in some cases, seen him play at dice for fifty dollars a throw and there were rumors of valuable ranches or an entire brand of cattle won or lost in a single poker game. They knew that he had borrowed or loaned thousands of dollars with no collateral involved except the name and reputation of the borrower.

"I've been doing business with you for some time now," an old ranchman once wrote to a friend who had met with misfortune. "We've bought and sold back and forth, and I think we're about even. You figure it up and if I owe you anything, let me know just what it is and I'll send you a check. If you owe me anything, just forget it." With such examples before him, it is not surprising that the cowboy was lavish with his money, nor is it strange that both he and his employer had nothing but contempt for the economic ideas of the settler. As a matter of fact, the business methods of the range area might be satisfactory enough so long as every one practiced them, but once brought into competition with the methods of the new society that was fast coming, they were nearly certain to bring ruin to those who could not or would not change.

If the range rider disliked the way of the pioneer settlers, however, the latter returned that dislike with full measure, "pressed down and running over." The cowboy had, of course, no fear of the homesteaders except the fear that their presence might threaten the security of the only business the ranchmen knew. The nesters, on the other hand, both feared and disliked the cowpuncher. To them the cowboy was a wild, reckless type who rode hard, swore hard, and feared neither God nor man. The nesters regarded the cowboy as a swaggering swashbuckler, who carried a gun, had little regard for horse flesh, and who seemed at all times to be "jealous of honor, sudden and quick in quarrel." He

probably never attended church or Sunday School and
would not, even if he had the chance. He spent his wages
foolishly and was strongly suspected of playing cards and
other sinful games. He wanted the region to remain a cow
country, favored "free grass," and would doubtless be glad
to see all the settlers "starve out" and depart for the region
whence they came. His ways were not their ways, nor his
thoughts their thoughts, and his interests were certainly not
their interests. The nesters wanted more settlers so that they
might have a school and preaching at least once or twice a
month as well as more and nearer neighbors. The cowboy
asserted the grass was the best crop this land would ever
produce and that the region would never be a thickly populated farming area; whereas on the hope that it would be
just that, the first settlers had well-nigh staked "their lives,
their fortunes, and their sacred honor." Eager for more neighbors, they wrote letters to friends and relatives in their old
home urging them to come west. Some yielded to their en-
treaties and came, occupying homesteads near those of the
firstcomers. Sod houses or dugouts sprang up—or down, as
the case might be—and little communities of settlers began to
be formed that were like small islands of crop growing in the
midst of the vast area of grazing lands that formed the pastoral empire of the Cow Country.

These small groups of settlers were but the advance agents
of a great population that was soon to follow. In the two
decades from 1870 to 1890, the population of the Dakotas
increased in round numbers from 14,000 to 719,000, that of
Nebraska from 122,000 to 1,058,000, Kansas from 364,000
to 1,427,000 and Texas from 818,000 to 2,235,000. Making
due allowance for inaccuracies in the census returns, these
figures are still truly startling, but the full significance of

this westward advance can be understood only after an examination of the census returns from some of the central and western counties of such states as Kansas and Nebraska, many of which show a population increase of a hundredfold in a single decade. During the next ten-year period, from 1890 to 1900, the increase in population in the western counties of the states mentioned and in the next tier of states to the west was also very great; while Oklahoma Territory with only sixty-one thousand people in 1890 had increased to four hundred thousand by 1900. Even in the first decade of the twentieth century Oklahoma, western Texas, and portions of other states in the range area show enormous increases in population.

Distrustful and contemptuous as the cowboy was of these earliest settlers upon the range, the time came when he could not entirely ignore them. Eventually the loneliness of life in his line camp or innate curiosity prompted him to stop at some homesteader's dugout or sod house to ask for a drink of water or to inquire about a stray horse. Here he in all probability made a discovery. The nester had a daughter—a comely young woman of eighteen or twenty years who, even though she belonged to a despised order, was nevertheless amazingly attractive! In a region where there were so few women, the coming of a new girl was regarded as an event of major importance. Too shy to talk much or remain long upon the occasion of his first visit, it was not many days until the cow hand returned bringing his offering in the form of half a quarter of fat beef, of uncertain origin, slung across his saddle.

The settler was suspicious of the Greeks when they came bearing gifts, but the family which had subsisted for weeks on a diet consisting largely of cornbread and buttermilk, warmed a bit to the giver. The wife urged that they could surely do no less than invite him to stay for supper. A kind of *entente cordiale* was established which, if tinged with distrust on both sides, did not perhaps differ so materially from similar arrangements made by nations of modern times. Away from the homesteader's family the cowpuncher sometimes felt a bit conscience stricken over his fall from grace and paid a visit to the daughter of some ranchman thirty miles away. Here he must meet the intense competition of a dozen other buckaroos and this, plus the memory of a pair of bright eyes, eventually brought him back to fraternize once more with this family outside his own caste.

The young woman's father spoke wisely and warningly of these wild cowboys and extolled in glowing terms the virtues of the hard-working farm boy on the adjoining claim, but it was plain that the daughter did not altogether agree with him. This is not surprising. After all, the callow granger lad in his overalls, ninety-eight cent wool hat, and heavy plow shoes did not compare favorably with a dashing figure on a spirited horse who rode a fifty-dollar saddle and wore ornate shop-made boots, "California trousers," a white Stetson hat, and soft gloves of the finest buckskin. As for the younger children of the household, they made no attempt to conceal their enthusiastic admiration. A man who could ride a bucking horse, rope a steer, and who carried a gun, wore jingling spurs, and gave you half a dollar merely for opening a gate for him was someone to admire! They compared the two-pound box of candy which he handed out so carelessly with the skimpy dime's worth brought from town by their father or the neighboring farm youth to be divided among four or five children, and it began to be plain where their affections lay.

It was not long before they began to imitate their hero. The father found his two younger sons trying to rope the dog with an improvised riata made from their mother's clothes line, or staging a rodeo back of the barn with the milk-pen calves playing the role of bucking broncos. They played cowboy and whittled pistols from wood long before a certain public enemy, who found such a contrivance useful, was born. Sent on an errand to the little store and post office that had been established in the new community, they lingered to listen to the conversation of the cow hands who had dropped in to inquire for the mail or to lay in a supply of tobacco. After remaining as long as they dared, the lads at last returned to their home with the best alibi they could muster and a vocabulary vastly enlarged even if not exactly enriched. The old songs brought from the East like the "Gypsy's Warning" and "Silver Threads Among the Gold," were apparently forgotten and the Sabbath stillness of the settler's home was shattered by such mournful productions as the "Dying Cowboy" or "Bury Me Not on the Lone Prairie." The mother, torn between a natural feminine love for a romantic figure and fears for her daughter's happiness, began in time to yield a somewhat reluctant admiration to a generous and attractive young man.

After several calls upon the young woman, the cowboy summoned up courage to ask her to accompany him to a dance, but unless in the northern zone of settlement where the German or Scandinavian element was large, he in all probability met with a courteous but uncompromising refusal. Dancing in many regions seems to lie at the two extremes of civilized society. The primitive and sophisticated both dance, but the in-betweens will have none of it. The girl made it plain that she was a member of the church and dancing was taboo. They were building a little schoolhouse in the neighborhood and expected to have preaching at least once a month. If he cared to go with her to church or literary society, or even to a social or play party at some settler's home, perhaps it could be arranged, but a dance was not to be considered. Even if she were willing to go, her parents would object and she was a dutiful and obedient daughter. So a play party or social it must be, attended largely by sons and daughters of the nesters. Here such games as "Miller Boy," "Down to Rowsers," and "Shoot the Buffalo" were played by the young people, while their fathers and mothers, who thought dancing the invention of the devil, looked on with smiling approbation. Later when the schoolhouse was finished, he accompanied her some Sunday to church and sat throughout the sermon in a state of painful self-consciousness which was considerably accentuated when she whispered to him her wish that he, too, might make "Heaven his destination."

As more settlers came in, the schoolhouse became something of a social center. Here were held singings, literary society meetings, and box suppers. At the last named, the boxes were sold at auction and young men would bid vociferously against one another for the box of some particularly attractive girl. After the boxes had all been sold, a cake was often given to the most popular young lady. Votes were usually one cent each, and in most cases there were but two leading candidates. One of these represented the range riders' interests—usually some ranchman's daughter who was clever and witty, an excellent dancer, and commonly known as "good company," whatever that might mean. In opposition to her the homesteaders would nominate a young woman who taught a Sunday School class, led the singing at church, and was known to be "good to wait on the sick." The two girls were conducted to the end of the room and seated near the teacher's desk where everyone could see the candidate for whom he was voting, and the contest began. As votes were called out and the money passed to the cashier, tellers checked on the blackboard the number of votes. In such cases the cowboys—even those who had shown some attention to a nester girl—usually rallied to the colors, while the granger lads and their fathers were equally determined to elect their nominee and vote *that girl* down! Eventually it became more than a contest between two personable young women. It was a conflict between two social and economic orders. To many of the settlers it was a struggle of the forces of evil against good, of darkness against light, of the past against the future. "Let us elect our candidate and prove to all that this is a progressive, God-fearing community, that the reign of the wild cowpuncher is over, that civilization is mighty and will prevail." Quite often the cow hands, who drew some thirty dollars a month in real money, were able to pay for more votes than could the poverty-stricken settlers. Reckless with their money as in all else, the range riders did not hesitate to pay out their last dollar for votes, but the homesteaders did their best, and if they went down in defeat they felt that this was merely another example of the triumph of might over right and of money over principles. They were certain that their day was coming and that it would not be long delayed.

In this they were not mistaken. Settlers continued to pour into the Cow Country in ever-increasing numbers and take up homesteads along the streams and in the more fertile areas of the wide prairies. The ranchmen were forced back into the rougher uplands sometimes remote from an adequate supply of water. Good land, however, produces good grass, while barren hills and thin soils afford poor grazing. For a time there still seemed to be an abundance of pasturage. The cowmen did not at first understand how much their range had suffered by the homesteading and fencing of the more fertile lowlands. Then they began to realize that their cattle did not fatten. They looked about for additional pasture lands, but they were not to be found. The range was steadily shrinking. Indian reservations were opened to settlement and a flood of homesteaders poured in, still further reducing the area that could be utilized for grazing. A village began to grow up about the first general store established in each community. Soon there came a second store, then a third, followed by a blacksmith shop, a hotel, and a church. Railroads began to penetrate the Cow Country and the village grew into a real town. Good land began to grow scarce. The homesteaders were soon very much in the majority in most parts of the Cow Country where there was sufficient rainfall for the growing of crops. Under such circumstances the fusion of the two social and economic orders went on rapidly. More and more cowpunchers began to call upon young women of the settler class. Dimly they began to comprehend how difficult it was for a man on a raw 160-acre claim to provide his family with the bare necessities of life. They saw the pitiful extremities to which the daughter of the household was driven to secure suitable clothing in order to keep herself attractive and to join in the social life of the community. Toleration took the place of the former antagonism and they began "first to endure, then pity, then embrace."

The homesteader, under the influence of closer association, found his prejudices beginning to melt. After all, these cowboys were not as bad as he had thought. Perhaps daughter might do worse. Unconsciously, his own conduct and psychology began to be at least slightly influenced by the customs of the range area. His horizon became wider. Finding he must travel greater distances than in the old home, he acquired another horse or two, secured a better saddle, and sometimes surprised his wife by the purchase of things formerly regarded as luxuries.

As the influx of settlers continued, church and school assumed a larger importance. An arbor was constructed and a revival meeting was held where cow hands who came to scoff sometimes remained to pray. Under the thundering sound of the minister's voice their thoughts turned to the sins of earlier days. They were strangely moved when the congregation sang "Almost Persuaded" or "Turn Sinners Turn," and they gazed with open-mouthed awe while the three-hundred-pound wife of a settler gave a solo rendition of "Love Lifted Me," thereby furnishing uncontrovertible proof of the power of redeeming love! Seeing how much a deep religious faith meant to people who must endure the hardships and vicissitudes of pioneer life, they sometimes sought in religion consolation for their own fast-multiplying troubles.

The ranchman, finding his range reduced, must purchase feed from the settlers or lease from them their surplus grazing land. Business relations once established paved the way for closer social relations. The old-time hostilities and prejudices were passing. There were, of course, bitter-enders in both groups who found their dislike of the other class only intensified by association, but they were in the minority. Generally speaking, the reverse was true. If the examples, given largely in terms of individuals or single communities, should be multiplied by several thousand, a fairly correct picture would be presented of the Cow Country in transition.

As more of the range was settled and plowed, the ranchman found he must reduce his herds and began to ship all merchantable cattle to market. The settlers, once they had secured a majority in the community, usually proceeded to vote a herd law which forced the ranchmen to acquire land in fee and enclose it with wire fences. With reduced herds and fenced pastures the rancher needed fewer men; cowboys of long experience found themselves out of a job and realized that it was impossible to secure one. Those retained, who had formerly scorned to do anything but ride, were forced to engage in such lowly work as building fences, plowing fireguards, and planting or harvesting forage crops —since with grazing lands so greatly reduced it had become necessary to feed cattle in winter. Some men out of employment rode farther west, seeking a region where they might hope to spend their lives in the cattle business, but it soon became apparent that there were not jobs enough for all. Many, especially those who had acquired a measure of tolerance for the new order, frankly accepted the changed conditions, married a nester girl, and took up a homestead. Here they grazed a few cattle, but it was not long before they began to plow and plant in awkward fashion and in time some became fairly successful farmers.

No doubt most of these marriages were happy ones, though it is possible that a larger proportion were not successful than in the case of marriages between persons of less widely divergent backgrounds. Such a statement is impossible to prove, though some evidence exists that it may be true. Texas, with a population of slightly more than three million in 1900, granted in the twenty-year period from 1887 to 1906 more than sixty-two thousand divorces, while Massachusetts, with a population of slightly less than three million in 1900, granted in the same twenty-year period fewer than twenty-three thousand, and Pennsylvania, with a population of more than six million, only thirty-nine thousand. Kansas, with a population of less than one and one-half million, had nearly twenty-nine thousand divorces in the period from 1887–1906, while New Jersey, with a considerably larger population, had fewer than eight thousand. Colorado had nearly sixteen thousand divorces in this twenty-year period, though the total population in 1900 was only slightly more than one-half million, while Connecticut, with a population nearly twice as great, had in round numbers only nine thousand. No doubt the greater ease with which divorce could be secured in a western state had its effect, but the very fact that divorce laws were more liberal in such states is in itself significant.

Not all cowboys who found their vocation gone would become farmers. Many who still hated the new order drifted to town seeking employment that would not put them into the class of the despised nesters. Three lines of business appealed to them and all three were doomed to speedy extinction. They could open a butcher shop in some small town, buying and slaughtering their own cattle; they could establish a livery stable and continue to work with horses; or they could open a saloon. With the coming of railroads and refrigerator cars, the great packing houses forced the local butchers out of business; the automobile destroyed the livery stable; and local option, and later prohibition, closed the saloon.

The ranchman fared no better in the midst of changed

conditions than did his cowpunchers. Some few who were wise accepted the inevitable, sold their cattle for what they would bring, bought a little land, and established a livestock farm. Others who were foolish tried to hold out as long as possible, borrowed money at ruinous rates of interest in order to rent pasturage or purchase feed, and in most cases lost everything. Their lax business methods might be satisfactory enough in a region where everyone else practiced the same code, but in a society which pinched pennies and drove hard bargains such methods could end only in disaster and financial ruin. The wrecks of many ranching enterprises that cover the onetime Cow Country give eloquent testimony as to how far this is true.

The desperation with which some ranchmen clung to the old order is little short of tragic. Like the Indians of the Ghost Dance who believed that the whites would vanish from the earth and the plains again be covered with buffalo, some of these men with an almost religious fervor held fast to the belief that the nesters would eventually return to the old homes whence they had come and that the region would once more become a pastoral empire as in days gone by. Their awakening came late, but in most cases it was thorough. Pasturage grew more and more restricted. Every portion of the range area suitable for crop growing—and much which it now seems was not suitable—was occupied. The cattle disappeared from the plains as if by magic and farmers armed with the tools of their craft sprang up on all sides as though some unseen hand had planted dragons' teeth on every hill and in every valley.

At last the cowman realized that the old order was gone and, in many cases, broken in fortune, he accepted the inevitable and set to work at strange tasks often with only his two hands with which to earn a living for himself and family. One who knows at first hand the story of these men is likely to forget their shortsightedness and poor judgment and to think only of their courage. Occasionally one of these men who has not yet accepted the new order may still be seen. Such an individual stands like a blackened tree trunk in the midst of plowed fields, a mute reminder of a bygone era. Janus like, he looks in two directions—toward an old world that has gone forever and toward a new one which he does not even remotely understand.

Though the Cow Country has passed away and the social order it produced is largely a memory, its influence throughout the region where that order once prevailed is still apparent. It is not mere accident that the University of Texas calls its magnificent dining hall the "Chuck Wagon" or that the walls of one of its finest buildings should display the old cattle brands of the Lone Star State, while a similar building at Harvard has carved beneath its eaves quotations from the Bible or from the classics. It is not by chance that traveling salesmen avidly read cowboy stories or that thousands of staid, sober citizens attend each year the rodeos held at many places in what was once the Cow Country. It is significant that Rotarians purchase from mail-order houses cowboy suits for their offspring and that thousands of people tune in each evening to hear some crooner render, with a Manhattan accent, "A Home on the Range" or "The Last Round-up." One finds a distinguished college professor decorating his office with a magnificent pair of steer horns and framed pictures of trail herds, roundup wagons, and other cowboy scenes. Throughout the West dude ranches have sprung up where college boys and girls, tired businessmen, and society matrons may, for a consideration, dress in leather chaps and ten-gallon hats and ride the range under suitable guidance, returning in the evening to eat from tin plates about a mess table and to sleep in a glorified bunk house.

Occasionally, in a more civilized society, a bit of the wild lawlessness of other days crops out as a reminder of the code of men long since dead. Old man Cow Country has gone, but his spirit still lives on in a generation that never knew him in the flesh. He was a good old man according to the green in the hearts of his descendants.

XI

The Cow Country and the Nation

Gone are the giant herds of yesterday,
Of long-horned Texas cattle, brown or dun,
The lean brown riders too have passed away.
Beneath the prairie's distant rim has sunk their sun;
Cattle and men who own them now are fat and white of face,
Their life is easy, it is better so;
And yet the passing years can never quite erase
The memory of those we knew so long ago.

THE LONGHORNS

THE ROMANTIC GLAMOUR THAT has clustered about the figure of the cowboy and about his land and work has served to obscure the real importance of ranching as a great productive industry of enormous significance in the history and life of the nation. It will be possible in a single, brief study only to point out a few of the more important aspects of the influence of the range cattle industry upon the life and development of the people of our country, leaving to others the task of giving in detail an account of each of them. Every one of the effects to be mentioned is well worthy of a lengthy paper involving extended and careful research, and when such studies are made they will in their entirety doubtless reveal how far we had hitherto overlooked the actual significance of the Cow Country in favor of its more picturesque and glamorous phases.

In the first place it should be observed that from the time the American colonists began to move from the Atlantic coast toward the interior of the continent, lines of travel, transportation, and communication always tended to run east and west. Not until the Mississippi was reached did they begin to extend north and south as the river trade and travel were developed, and after the first tier of states beyond that stream had been occupied such lines began once more to follow the older pattern. Well-known examples are the Mormon trail to Utah, the route to Oregon, and the trails broken by the Argonauts seeking the golden treasures of California. Only the Santa Fe Trail angled off to the Southwest but even it was far more nearly a road to and from the West than the South since it in time became only the first part of a southern route to California.

Along these east and west trails broken by the first emigrants there soon developed a considerable traffic as various transportation companies like that of Russell, Majors and Waddell began freighting goods to California. The overland stage, pony express, and telegraph lines quickly followed and it was not many years until transcontinental lines of railway linked the Mississippi with the Pacific Ocean. In this trans-Mississippi West, however, there were for many years virtually no lines of either travel or trade running north and south.

The great drives of Texas cattle cut across these east and west routes of transportation and communication and for the first time brought into contact the North and South of the trans-Mississippi area. Men of Texas and Kansas came together with results described in a previous chapter, and later the trails extended on to the far North linking the Texas ranchmen with those of the northern plains.

Despite the hostility that grew up between Texas and Kansas, friction by no means always resulted from such regional contacts. On the contrary they often resulted in a better understanding out of which grew co-operation, mutual helpfulness, and a certain fusion of interests. The northern plainsmen soon came to look to Texas as a source of supply for stocker cattle and the latter area found in the region farther north a market for the surplus animals of their fast-increasing herds. While interests were occasionally divergent, the cattle growers of the northern and southern plains soon found that they had many common problems which they sought to solve by means of intelligent co-operation. These included such matters as the occupation of the public domain, opening of credit channels to the East, improving the breeds of cattle on the ranges, the promotion of foreign trade, the securing of favorable legislation, and the prevention, if possible, of the passage of laws detrimental to the livestock growers. Other matters of common interest had to do with range and water conservation, fencing, favorable freight rates for rail shipments, checking depredations upon livestock, and the improvement of marketing facilities by the creation of adequate stockyards. The establishment of these north and south highways over which cattle were driven undoubtedly brought northern and southern ranchmen closer together and helped to promote a spirit of co-operation and to unify the vast empire of grass which was the Cow Country.

Of further far-reaching importance was the fact that just as the early wagon trails extending westward across the plains paved the way for the Pacific Railway, so did these cattle trails leading to the north influence the building of great trunk lines of railway from the North to the Southwest. The Missouri-Kansas-Texas was the first built primarily to tap the great reservoir of Texas cattle. It was quickly followed by the Santa Fe and the Rock Island, both seeking to secure a share of the livestock shipments from Texas and the Southwest. All of these lines followed roughly the old cattle trails and their chief freight business for many years consisted of shipments of livestock. Yet they, in common with other lines, opened up the plains to occupation by settlers, and as crop growing began to take the place of ranching, a large freight business was developed in cotton, wheat, agricultural machinery, lumber, household goods, and general merchandise. There can be no doubt that the development of the range cattle industry was of primary importance in promoting the early building of railway lines to the Southwest as well as throughout the Great Plains as a whole and that such railroads made possible the occupation of enormous areas of prairie land by farmers.

The cattlemen themselves, moreover, were the advance agents of the homesteaders and pointed the way to the occupation of much of the Great West by settlers. This was particularly true with respect to the great Indian reservations of western Oklahoma and in some other western states and Territories. Large tracts of land were set aside for the use of Indian tribes and white occupation of them was forbidden. It was as though a dike or wall had been erected about these Indian lands by governmental decree. The ranchmen asserted, however, that they had no interest in the land itself, but only in the pasturage which it afforded and that their utilization of this would in no way affect the Indian's use of his reservation or his title to its soil. In time an industry more fluid in character than is agriculture in the ordinary sense of the term began to penetrate this dike and to spread itself over the pasture lands within. The result might easily have been foreseen. Farmers living along the reservation borders who saw cattlemen pasturing herds on Indian lands, enclosing them with wire fences and erecting line camps and corrals, loudly asserted that here was a form of unjust discrimination. They could see no reason why wealthy cattlemen should be allowed to enter upon Indian reservations, graze their herds there, and derive large profits from native pasturage while farmers, in need of homes and desiring to grow corn and wheat, should be excluded. In some instances they sought to occupy such lands by force in defiance of law and the regulations of the Indian Bureau. While unsuccessful in this, their clamor, swelled by that of their friends and well-wishers, eventually became so great that Congress was forced to yield and open these reservations to white settlement. While this would in time have been done even if the ranchmen had never occupied such Indian lands with their herds, it is certain that it was greatly hastened by such occupation.

Though the influence of the range cattle business in promoting the settlement of the public domain is less apparent than in the case of Indian lands, it was none the less very real. Would-be settlers who had hesitated to go far out upon the prairies and take a homestead saw there a scattering population of ranchmen. Some of these were cutting hay or growing gardens, thus revealing, to a certain extent, the agricultural possibilities of the soil. If the ranchmen could live there and prosper, the settlers reasoned that they could do so as well. They began to occupy homesteads in various portions of the Cow Country and their advance was cumulative, each pioneer settler being followed by his relatives, friends, and former neighbors. As railroads began to penetrate the range area the movement of these settlers westward became a torrent which in a few years was to overwhelm the ranchmen and to turn much of the former Cow Country into a crop-growing region of homes, towns, and cities.

As has been previously indicated, however, the ranchmen did not yield without a struggle and the contest which developed between the two economic and social orders was

not without nationwide significance. To many a poor homesteader the important cattleman was the representative of
wealth and aristocracy, and the large ranching firms which
sought to control the range were the first corporations and
the only monopolies that he had ever known. His hostility
toward them paved the way for a feeling of hostility against
all forms of corporate wealth and capitalism in general. So
were sown the seeds of Populism in the prairie West.

The relations which developed quite early between the
range area and the Corn Belt were also of far-reaching importance. Such corn-growing states as Missouri, Iowa, Illinois, Indiana, and some others had before the Civil War
largely produced their own feeder cattle. This meant that a
considerable number of breeding animals must be retained at
all times in order to produce the steers to be fattened for
slaughter. Under such circumstances large areas of land potentially valuable for corn growing must be devoted to pasturage or the growth of hay. Once the Cow Country began
to supply these states with an ample supply of feeders the
breeding of beef cattle could largely be given up and much of
this former pasture and meadowland plowed and planted to
corn. From this time on feeders were obtained largely from
the western ranges and such breeding as continued in the
corn-growing states was primarily of registered animals to be
sold to ranchmen to improve the quality of their herds. Since
it is far more profitable to feed well-bred animals than scrubs,
the Corn Belt was vitally interested in improving the quality
of the cattle raised on the Great Plains. Many stock farms developed in these corn-growing states specializing in the production of registered bulls to be sold to the western ranchmen. The calves of these sires when two years old were then
often shipped to the Corn Belt to be fattened for market.

Yet, though the number of registered cattle bred in the corn-growing region was greatly increased, the total number of animals bred in that area was much less than in former times when these farmers largely produced their own feeder cattle. Because of large acreage, corn production in these states was vastly increased in the two decades between 1870 and 1890.

The influence of the Cow Country upon the foreign trade has already been discussed with some detail. This trade, of course, greatly stimulated both feeding and breeding since the British market demanded fat, heavy beef of highest quality which grass-fed Texas cattle could not supply. The shipment of dressed beef to Europe, however, had other consequences no less significant. It created an interest in cattle raising on the plains in the British Isles and brought many millions of dollars of British capital to America for investment in ranching enterprises. It also brought many Scots and Englishmen to western America who in some cases remained to engage in other business after the range cattle industry in its larger sense was a thing of the past. Ships carrying beef from America to England returned with cargoes of manufactured goods. Trade relations between the two countries were promoted and as shipments of beef and cattle declined other agricultural products or raw materials took their place. It seems certain that the Cow Country was a considerable factor in the promotion of American foreign trade and the opening up of new markets for American products.

While the relationships established between ranchmen and the corn growers of the midwestern states were of vital importance to both of these regions, those which developed between the range area and the cotton-producing states of the deep South were also of considerable consequence.

As the great stream of Texas cattle pouring northward up the long trails grew in volume, it became clear to many ranchmen of the Lone Star State that even their apparently inexhaustible supply of animals would not always be sufficient to meet the demands of the northern ranges. Despite an enormous annual calf crop, the Texans discovered that they could hardly produce animals as fast as this northern market could absorb them. Looking about for a source from which additional cattle might be drawn, they found it in these cotton states to the east.

Most of the farmers in these states owned a few milk cows which, together with numerous small herds pastured on the rougher lands unfit for cotton growing, gave to the region as a whole a very considerable number of cattle. For any surplus there was little market until one was discovered in the range area of the southern plains. Finding that the northern market was apparently unlimited, many Texas ranchmen began to go into eastern Texas, Arkansas, Louisiana, Mississippi, Alabama, and even at times as far east as Georgia, to purchase herds of these cattle. The animals were in many cases "milk pen calves" and the steer calves from such small herds as these southern stock farmers pastured in the wooded hills on land that could not be profitably cultivated. They were usually small and of inferior quality but once brought to the Great Plains they increased surprisingly in flesh and weight on the rich buffalo grass of that region. They, together with cattle from the Texas coast area, were often called "dogies," a term commonly applied in loose fashion to any small cattle. By providing the so-called "Cotton Belt" with a market for its surplus cattle, the range area affected to an appreciable degree the economic life of the cotton farmers of that region.

Even more important, however, was the market which the Cow Country afforded the cotton growers for the great by-product of their chief crop. This was cottonseed and cottonseed meal, or cake. For many years cottonseed had no value whatever. Thousands of tons were dumped into the Mississippi or other rivers merely in order to be rid of it. With the discovery of the value of cottonseed oil and the erection of mills to produce it, a commodity formerly regarded as entirely worthless suddenly became of great commercial importance. Yet, in the period when such mills were few and far between and before the use of cottonseed oil and its products had become so nearly universal, hundreds of thousands of tons of raw cottonseed were shipped westward for feeding cattle in the range area. Later, cottonseed meal, or cake, a far more concentrated food, began to be utilized by feeders in fattening cattle for market. Even the hulls were used as roughage and the price of cottonseed eventually rose to such heights that the increased value of a bale of cotton owing to the market for the seed sometimes represented the only margin of profit to the farmer who grew it. The utilization of cottonseed and cottonseed meal by the livestock growers as feed for cattle undoubtedly brought millions of dollars to the cotton-growing states during the period of the range cattle industry.

The rise of the Cow Country undoubtedly had a powerful influence upon the growth of the meat-packing industry. The great packing plants established at Chicago, Kansas City, Fort Worth, and various other market centers were colossal in size compared with such earlier establishments as were built at Cincinnati, Cleveland, Louisville, and a number of other towns and cities farther east. These earlier enterprises received their animals for slaughter largely from livestock growers on farms in midwestern states. The newer plants in the fast-growing cities farther west looked to the Cow Country as the original source of a large part of their cattle though many of these were first shipped from the range area to the Corn Belt to be fed for six months or more before consignment to market for slaughter. Hogs were placed in the feed lots with these cattle to consume the grain that would otherwise have been wasted, and these also served to swell the volume of business done by the packers. These establishments eventually became so large that they could operate with a maximum degree of efficiency. Not only did they utilize every part of the animal but also began the manufacture of butter, cheese, soap, fertilizer, and many other products. Their large-scale operations and the enormous supply of animals afforded by the range area undoubtedly made beef cheaper both in the United States and Great Britain than it had formerly been. Consumption was thus increased since many people could afford to purchase more meat than they had formerly been able to. Range production plus efficient operation of great packing plants put beef on the tables of many laborers in industrial centers of the East in far more generous quantities than ever before.

The spread of ranching over the plains and the growing importance of the business fostered scientific experimentation which in time resulted in many new discoveries and inventions of great importance to the nation and to the world. Long and careful study of the cause and nature of Texas, or splenetic, fever, following heavy losses from the dread disease, resulted in the discovery that it was a malady to which southern cattle are immune, but which they carried to animals farther north by means of the so-called "fever ticks." Further experiments showed how the parasites could be destroyed by "dipping" the cattle in vats filled with a creosote mixture. In this way and by stringent quarantine regulations and the erection of separate stockyards for southern cattle, the disease was brought under control and in time largely eliminated. This saved hundreds of thousands of dollars annually not only to ranchmen but to livestock growers in the crop-growing regions farther east. Other studies resulted in the vaccination of cattle against blackleg and additional scientific measures for the prevention and cure of disease.

The spread of the range cattle industry was also largely responsible for the invention of barbed wire, which was the outgrowth of experiments directed toward providing a cheap and efficient means of enclosing large areas of pasture lands on the plains. Few inventions have been of greater consequence. Originally designed and manufactured for the convenience of the Cow Country, its use as fencing material in time spread over the country as a whole. Also, barbed wire eventually became of utmost importance in military defense and has been used by the armies of virtually every great nation in the world.

The fact that large areas of the Great Plains were unwatered brought a great advance in the improvement of machinery for the drilling of deep wells in order to make these lands available for grazing. It seems probable that the drilling of such wells and the perfecting of new methods in such work may have been of some significance in pointing the way to more efficient drilling of oil wells later in the mid-continent field.

The growing scarcity of range and the necessity for feeding cattle during the winter months undoubtedly promoted the world-wide search by agricultural experts for drought-resisting crops that might be grown on the semiarid plains of much of the range area. Unquestionably the widespread growth of kaffir, milo, African millet, and the Johnson grass so cordially hated by many farmers has been in a great measure brought about by the necessity for providing forage for cattle in the range states. Some of these crops, however, have continued to be very important in many areas from which ranching in the ordinary and older sense of the term has long since disappeared.

The influences of the Cow Country so briefly mentioned have not only in most cases extended to every part of the United States but not a few of them have reached Europe as well. But there are other and more intangible effects of the development of livestock growing on the western plains that are no less significant to American life. One of these was the creation of a Cow Country psychology or, if specialists in that field of study object to such use of the word, the development of a state of mind or cultural heritage which has persisted long after the conditions and the life which produced it have passed away. The range rider was a type. The nature of his work demanded initiative, courage, resourcefulness, loyalty, and a sense of humor. Often remote from human contacts, he must make his own decisions with respect to the solution of numerous pressing and important problems. A strong sense of personal independence inevitably followed though he was at times often forced to adopt co-operative measures and must learn to work with others for the common good. He was essentially a man of action, yet in the long, lonely hours spent in the saddle or in his remote line camp, there was ample time and opportunity for uninterrupted thought. Eventually he developed an unconscious philosophy of life or, more correctly perhaps, an attitude toward life. If a problem could be solved or a danger averted by action, that action must be prompt and decisive. On the other hand "what could not be cured must be endured" and it was far better to endure it with cheerfulness and good humor. Certainly the difficulties and discomforts created by sleet, snow, drought, and flood could not be overcome by complaints or railing against the weather. It was far better to joke and laugh about them and not lose hope for the future.

In this way his attitude was not unlike that of the soldier expressed in the lines of the one time popular song:

> *What's the use to worry? It never was worth while.*
> *So pack up your troubles in your old kit bag*
> *And smile, smile, smile.*

There was, however, a notable difference between the two. The soldier feels that there is no need to worry because he has no control over his own actions. Always there is a superior officer near to tell him exactly what to do and how to do it. On the other hand, the very essence of range life was individualism. The cow hand must decide for himself concerning his actions and must develop skill and a large measure of versatility in meeting difficult situations.

As a matter of fact, there was neither sympathy nor understanding between range riders and the cavalrymen garrisoning the frontier army posts. Cowboys out of a job who were asked if they had ever considered enlisting in the army threw up their hands in dismay at the suggestion. The thought of military discipline, red tape, and of being subject to army regulations was to them abhorrent. So long as they lived they meant to retain their own personal freedom. Complete democracy and the absence of anything approaching a caste system was the ideal of the cow hand. Birth, rank, position, or wealth meant to him very little. "I'm no better," said Tom Smith, of the Circle S, "than anybody else that's respectable, but I want the world to know that I'm just as good as any man that ever rode a hoss or walked the ground." This attitude was well-nigh universal among the range riders.

Another characteristic of these men was a tendency to despise anything in the nature of sham, pretense, or snobbishness. This has been true of most people in the pioneer West but the nature of range life was such as to strip off all pose or pretense and reveal every individual in his true colors. It has been said that one comes to know a man far better on a week's camping trip than in many years of ordinary business association. Certainly a dozen men who set out to drive a herd of cattle from Texas to Montana knew one another very well indeed before the end of a journey lasting four or five months. Also two line riders who spent a winter together in some dugout camp thirty miles from any other human habitation had few illusions about each other by the time spring had come. All frailties and weaknesses in common with every strong, generous, and kindly impulse were speedily discovered and fully recognized. Men came to be judged by their own personal qualities and by what they could do rather than measured by any such irrelevant standards as family, education, or property. The cowboys were, moreover, not slow to point out to a companion his faults and weaknesses. This was in no sense the manifestation of a missionary spirit, for the range rider was no missionary. He recognized, however, that an incompetent individual and above all one who was selfish and disagreeable, or who sought to shirk his duties, made it difficult for others who must work with him. Such a man had no place in the Cow Country and usually did not remain there long. Either he learned how to do his work well and did it cheerfully and wholeheartedly, or his life soon became so unbearable that he left the range to seek elsewhere a more congenial atmosphere.

Perhaps the most distinguishing trait of the range rider was loyalty. This went far beyond his loyalty to the interests of his employer or the brand which for the time being had become his own coat of arms, though this was intense and sincere. Primarily, however, it was a loyalty to his vocation, to the traditions, or the code and ideals, of the Cow Country. It was this which kept him in the saddle in subzero weather despite snow and sleet and the bitter north winds of the high plains. Because of it he faced death by stampeding cattle and vicious horses, or at the hands of human enemies, almost daily without flinching. A man must at all times be a man regardless of consequences. He must always be generous in helping others and never under any circumstances turn his back on a friend or a foe. Such was the law of the range and toward it the cowboy maintained an unswerving loyalty.

All of these characteristics of the range riders when taken in the aggregate eventually served to give to the regional society which they formed a certain intangible quality that might be designated as the Spirit of the Cow Country. First on the ground as they were, the ranchmen and their riders transmitted a certain measure of this spirit to those people who later came among them to establish farms and build towns and cities. Moreover, as the range cattle industry declined and many men formerly engaged in it scattered throughout the country to enter new vocations, they carried this spirit with them wherever they went. Its influence upon others must not be overemphasized but they could hardly fail to pass it on in some degree to their children as well as to spread its ideals among their neighbors and associates as a leaven which in time came to affect the points of view and attitudes of people in every walk of life.

The influence of this spirit has been kept alive and rendered far more widespread by the last of the effects of the range area upon the nation to be mentioned. This is the creation and development of a distinctive literature of the Cow Country. Almost from the very first the life of the livestock growers on the western plains has served to stimulate the imagination not only of those who shared in it or knew something of it at first hand, but of many others as well. Joseph G. McCoy, Andy Adams, John Clay, Eugene Manlove Rhodes, and many other men formerly engaged in ranching have given us fascinating books on the life which they knew so well.

On the whole, however, most cowboys and ranchmen were either too busy with their chosen work to spend much time in writing or else lacked the literary skill necessary to put on paper an account of their experiences and adventures. Others, however, were not slow to capitalize on the possibilities offered by the far-reaching public interest in a picturesque and romantic vocation carried on in a picturesque and romantic region. As a result, literally millions of pages have been published and widely read dealing with every aspect of the range cattle industry and ranch life. This literature includes everything from highly technical studies prepared with painstaking care by well-trained research scholars to the lightest of featherweight fiction penned by men and women without the slightest knowledge, or conception, of the subject of which they wrote. Yet, each kind had its readers, and as the range cattle business steadily declined in importance, the volume of material published about it seemed steadily to increase. Many excellent books of fiction and numerous short stories dealing with the Cow Country have appeared and some of these were not only best sellers but bid fair to take and hold a place as classics in American literature. The moving-picture companies, quick to take advantage of every opportunity, began the production of "westerns" in many cases dealing with ranch life and have released a large number of good films of that character. Cowboy songs became popular, and certain western artists like Frederic Remington, Charles M. Russell, and Will James have given us pictures that lead to a better understanding of cowboys and range life than it is possible to secure through the printed page alone.

The result of all this has been that millions of people have come to share in vicarious fashion the life of the former Cow Country and to understand and appreciate in some small measure at least its spirit and ideals. Many, if not most, of these never saw the plains or mounted a horse and yet this knowledge of range life acquired in such secondhand fashion could hardly fail to influence their own attitudes and ideals. Many a growing lad has doubtless had his own conduct shaped through his thoughts of what the "Lone Rider," "Red Ranger," or some other favorite character of fiction or the screen would have done under similar circumstances.

The volume of this literature, moreover, seems to increase rather than lessen with the passing years, and the end of popular interest in ranch life as it existed a generation ago appears very remote. It is certain that if it were possible to enumerate the clock hours spent in riding the range by all the men who shared in the work of the Cow Country, the number secured would be far less than that obtained by enumerating the hours spent by people in reading cowboy

stories and viewing on the screen what modern youth flip-
pantly calls "horse operas." In consequence, the cow hand
has steadily grown in stature as a legendary figure even as
his importance as a real person was steadily declining.

The period of the range cattle industry constitutes the heroic age in the history of the West and like every other
heroic age it has a deep interest for later generations. While
it is true that most of this interest has been in its more romantic and colorful phases and that this has served to blind
us to its tangible effects upon the economic history and life
of our people, yet it seems probable that not the least of
the contributions of the Cow Country to the nation has been
the creation and development of one distinctive type of
American literature, which still does not seem to have reached
its full flowering even though the life which produced it
has gone forever.

To state that the life described in the literature of the Cow
Country has disappeared does not in any sense, however,
imply that ranching, or the production of cattle largely upon
native pasturage, has vanished or even declined. As a matter
of fact, it is probably more important today than at any
time in the past. Only the former life, and not the cattle industry itself, has passed away. The 1940 census indicated
that Oklahoma had, at that time, in round numbers, 2,300,000
head of cattle; unquestionably far more than at the time when
the range cattle industry was at the zenith of its importance.
No doubt the same was true of virtually every other of the
so-called grazing states. But the Cow Country as a distinct
entity is gone, and the social and economic pattern which
characterized it has largely vanished. Only in a few regions
too rough or arid for successful crop growing may still be
found something reminiscent of the old-time order. Even

here, however, there are many marked differences and the life at its best, or worst, depending upon the point of view, is only a more or less faded and imperfect copy of that which exists in the memories of the few remaining range riders of long ago.

A large part of the former range area is now a thickly populated region of farms, towns, and cities where crop growing, commerce, and industry have created a society entirely unlike that produced by the crude pastoral economy of earlier years. Modern means of transportation have affected the livestock industry very much. Cattle are moved by truck or train instead of over long trails on their own feet and under their own power. The old Texas longhorns have been replaced by fat, blocky, well-bred animals, owned and cared for by college-trained men skilled in the technical details of breeding, feeding, marketing, range conservation, and all other aspects of their business. This steady advance in scientific methods of beef production has been in progress for many years and will doubtless continue until the last, lingering traces of the old-time days and ways will have completely disappeared from even those remote areas where to some extent they still persist.

Yet the traditions and ideals of the former range riders and their once powerful empire will for a long time remain to influence and color the pattern of American life. The romantic figure of the cowboy will for generations continue to gallop across countless printed pages to thrill the hearts of a great multitude of readers who never knew him in the flesh. More important perhaps, it seems probable that many a modern ranchman who traverses his pasture lands in a powerful motor car in order to inspect his cattle, and who practices the most recent of scientific methods in their care, may find in a study of the history of his pioneer forebears something of real value to him in carrying on his own business. Even though conditions may have changed so radically as to make earlier methods largely impracticable today, the story of the loyalty and devotion of these early cattlemen to their chosen vocation and of the resourcefulness and courage with which they faced their many difficult problems must prove a source of inspiration to every present-day livestock raiser.

THIS EDITION OF *Cow Country* HAS BEEN PRINTED ON
PAPER EXPECTED TO LAST THREE HUNDRED YEARS

UNIVERSITY OF OKLAHOMA PRESS
NORMAN

Dale, Edward Everett, 1879-
  Cow country. [New ed.]   Norman, University
of Oklahoma Press [1965]
  258p. illus. 20cm.   (The Western frontier
library [no.27])

257605

1.Frontier and pioneer life—The West. 2.Cowboys.
3.Cattle trade—The West. I.Title. II.Series:The Western
frontier library, v.27.